How To Find Your Wealthy Place

by
Dr. Leroy Thompson Sr.

Ever Increasing Word Ministries
Darrow, Louisiana

Unless otherwise indicated, all Scripture quotations in this volume are from the *King James Version* of the Bible.

First Printing 1999

ISBN 0-963-2584-5-1

Ever Increasing Word Ministries
P.O. Box 7
Darrow, Louisiana 70725

Contents

It has been my God-given privilege as well as my responsibility for several years now to teach believers about divine prosperity and, in particular, about money and how we can have more of it *God's way.*

This revelation concerning the wealthy place is perhaps one of the strongest messages I've received since "Money cometh." Step by step, the Lord has shown me how to show you God's will and His plan for your financial prosperity. There are real steps we can take and real results we should receive when we take those steps.

The Lord told me, "Leroy, I have given you a voice for money, and I have given My people ears to hear. I have anointed you to get the truth across to My people. They are going to get it this time like never before. Keep the vision clear. Keep the revelation clear. Do not compromise. Do not apologize. This time I will not be denied."

The most valuable truth you can learn about your Heavenly Father is that He is a good, loving Father who has made every provision for you to have everything you need pertaining to life and godliness (2 Peter 1:3). This foundation of knowing and understanding that God is a good God and Father must be laid before a person can enter in to what I call "Ephesians 3:20 abundance" — more than he can ask or think!

In the wealthy place — in *your* wealthy place, because every believer has a wealthy place in God — there is not only abundant financial prosperity, but a full, rich walk with God besides. God has blessed us to make us a blessing. But how many of us are satisfied with where we are in the arena of being a blessing to others?

No matter where you are today — in the land of "not enough," the land of "just enough," or the land of "more than enough," God wants to do more for you. Actually, the problem with most people in the area of finances is not a lack of money. It's a lack of understanding concerning all that God wants to do for them financially.

There is a place you can go to where you do not have to even think about money, because you have so much of it. And every believer, not just a select few, can go there.

God has brought me into my wealthy place, but I do not want to hide my blessing or keep silent about what the Lord has done for me. I don't want to be satisfied to be blessed — just "me and my four and no more." I want the Body of Christ to move up higher in their finances, and I want God's glory to be seen as they do. I believe that now, more than ever before, is the time for that to happen.

There Is a Wealthy Place in God

God wants to bring you into a wealthy place — into your very own wealthy place in Him. Your entering into that place is going to affect your finances and every area of your life for good. God has brought me into a wealthy place personally and in my ministry, and I want to show you how you can find *your* wealthy place.

God said in Deuteronomy 28:3, **"Blessed shalt thou be in the city, and blessed shalt thou be in the field."** You see, it works in the city and in the field. In other words, whether you are a doctor, lawyer, school teacher, minister, or you have some other vocation, what I am about to show you will work for you.

In teaching on this subject, it is crucial that you understand that God will not *drive* you into a wealthy place; He will only *lead* you. God will not force you to prosper financially. So you have to learn how to find your wealthy place and then *let* God bring you there.

Let's look at Psalm 66:12, which is my golden text.

Thou hast caused men to ride over our heads; we went through fire and through water: BUT THOU BROUGHTEST US OUT INTO A WEALTHY PLACE.
PSALM 66:12

Let's look at the first part of this verse: **"Thou hast caused men to ride over our heads; we went through fire and through water...."** You know, all of us at some time or another have gone through hard places — through fire and through water — financially. We've been in some tight spots, so to speak. But the good news is, it is God's will that we come out of those places! In other words, we don't have to stay there in those tight spots financially!

Some people have lived for years in hard places financially, because they have not known that they could come out. But God wants to bring them out of the mess they're in financially.

'Out' and 'Into'

Let me show you something about the Lord from Psalm 66:12. It says, **"Thou hast caused men to ride over our heads; we went through fire and through water: but thou broughtest us OUT INTO a wealthy place."**

The Lord never does anything halfway. In other words, His intention is never to bring someone *out* of something without bringing him or her *into* something better. We saw that in the case of the children of Israel when God brought them out of Egypt's bondage and into their Promised Land. And in Psalm 66:12 we see that God brought His people out of the "fire and water" and into a wealthy place.

Have you ever been through the "fire and water" concerning money? Many have had problems with money all their lives — and their problem was they didn't have any — and they've just accepted it. But we've accepted some things we shouldn't have accepted. We've classified them as normal. But it is not normal to be broke; it is abnormal. However, Psalm 66:12 says, **"Thou hast caused men to ride over our heads; we went through fire and through water: BUT thou broughtest us out into a wealthy place"**!

Today Is the Day — Now Is the Time

I believe the following verse in Psalms is a prophetic word to the Body of Christ for this hour concerning finances.

Thou shalt arise, and have mercy upon Zion: for the time to favour her, yea, the set time, is come.
PSALM 102:13

I like the first three words, **"Thou shalt arise...."** They do me good! With all my heart, I believe there is a set time for the Church to rise up in the area of prosperity, and I believe that this is the time.

Now don't misunderstand me. It *has been*, *is*, and *always will be* God's will for His people to prosper. But more than ever before, I believe that now is the time God wants to show off His children to the world and cause them to take their places in Christ — and that includes taking their places in financial prosperity.

> **Thou shalt arise, and have mercy upon ZION: for the time to favour her, yea, the set time, is come.**
> **PSALM 102:13**

Zion is a type of the Church. When God talks about Zion, He is prophetically speaking about the Church of the Lord Jesus Christ. The last part of Psalm 102:13 says, **"... for the time to favour her** [Zion, or the Church], **yea, the set time, is come."** As a Christian, as a member of the Church of Jesus Christ, you can confidently say, "The time for my favor has come. I am opening up to God's favor. I have tried to do things myself, but I could not. I am going to let Him bring me 'out' and 'into.'"

Well, what is He going to bring you out *into*? This day is the set time of our favor when God is going to arise and bring us into a wealthy place!

I want you to get it in your consciousness that this money message is a "right-now" message. God wants His people to experience financial breakthroughs right now — today — on the earth, before Jesus comes back. Jesus is not coming back for a broke, defeated, and looking-for-a-handout Church.

You need to continually remind yourself that your life today is in the "time zone" of God's favor. You need to believe that now is your "set time" — not tomorrow or next month or next year, but right now.

To enable God to bring you into a wealthy place, first, you will have to become personally acquainted with your covenant — with the covenant that He has provided for you in Christ. And that covenant is a covenant of wealth.

Plans, Purposes, Designs, and Objectives

Second, you have to know that God deals with plans, purposes, designs, and objectives. God has a plan for you as His child to be wealthy; God has a purpose for you to be wealthy; God has a design for you to be wealthy; and God has an objective for you to be wealthy. If you don't understand that, you might think the prosperity message is about selfishly "grabbing" for more and more when, in actuality, the Father has plans, purposes, designs, and objectives for His people to be wealthy.

Kingdom business will be taken care of through God's people. And in the process of God's people taking care of Kingdom business, the Kingdom will have to take care of them properly. In other words, God's plan, purpose, design, and objective is to have you take care of Kingdom business with your finances. Then at the same time, because of your covenant relationship with Him as your Heavenly Father, He wants to take care of you in a certain style.

God did that very thing for Ruth in the Old Testament. When Ruth's husband died, Ruth had every right to return to her own people. Yet she stuck with her mother-in-law Naomi and went to a strange land with her. The next thing you know, Ruth meets up with a very wealthy, aristocratic man and eventually marries him. One minute Ruth was broke, and the next minute, she was living in a palace (*see* the Book of Ruth)!

Ruth was faithful. She took care of Kingdom business by sticking with her mother-in-law when she could have chosen the comforts of home — of being surrounded by her own family and friends. Ruth sought the true and living God instead of the gods her people served. And God blessed her tremendously as a result.

When you know what God's will is and you're walking with Him and developing a personal relationship with Him, you are putting yourself in position for Him to take care of you financially in the way that He wants to. You are enabling Him to "release" His part of the covenant on your behalf.

Ignorance of God's Word Is Not 'Bliss'

Many good, well-meaning Christians desire to have an in-depth knowledge of God and His Word and to wholeheartedly do His will. But they are hindered in the area of prosperity. They have been willing and obedient (Isa. 1:19), yet they have missed it concerning money. There are several reasons why they are not prospering as they should. One main reason is, many do not even know that there is a wealthy place in God.

Many Christians have no idea that there is a wealthy place in God that He wants to bring them into. When I say "wealthy place," I'm talking about money. I know that there are other aspects of being wealthy. For example, you could be rich in good health. You could be rich in the fruit of the spirit — in love, joy, peace, longsuffering, and so forth. But when I talk about the wealthy place that God wants to bring you into, I'm talking about finances.

What Is the Will of the Lord?

I see many who aren't missing it in the area of the fruit of the spirit, but they are missing it in the area of money. The reason for that is, largely, they do not understand the will of the Lord.

Wherefore be ye not unwise, but understanding
WHAT THE WILL OF THE LORD IS.

EPHESIANS 5:17

What is the will of the Lord? Well, the will of the Lord
includes financial prosperity.

Beloved, I wish above all things that thou mayest
prosper and be in health, even as thy soul
prospereth.

3 JOHN 2

Actually, three types of prosperity are talked about
here: prosperity in your *health*; prosperity in your
finances; and prosperity in your *soul*.

God's will for you is financial prosperity. I can
further prove that by the Word.

But thou shalt remember the Lord thy God: for it is
he that giveth thee power to get wealth, that he
may establish his covenant which he sware unto
thy fathers, as it is this day.

DEUTERONOMY 8:18

Praise ye the Lord. Blessed is the man that feareth
the Lord, that delighteth greatly in his
commandments.

His seed shall be mighty upon earth: the
generation of the upright shall be blessed.
Wealth and riches shall be in his house: and his
righteousness endureth for ever.

PSALM 112:1-3

For the Lord God is a sun and shield: the Lord will
give grace and glory: no good thing will he
withhold from them that walk uprightly.

PSALM 84:11

The Lord is my shepherd; I shall not want.

PSALM 23:1

In the Twenty-Third Psalm, David also said, **"Thou
preparest a table before me in the presence of mine
enemies: thou anointest my head with oil; MY CUP
RUNNETH OVER"** (v. 5).

I believe that if God did that for David, He'll do it for
you!

I think you can see from the Word that God doesn't
have a problem with your being wealthy. In fact, wealth is
what He wants for you!

Let's look at Deuteronomy again at a description of
the wealthy place God wants to bring you into.

> For the Lord thy God bringeth thee into a good land, a land of brooks of water, of fountains and depths that spring out of valleys and hills.
>
> **DEUTERONOMY 8:7**

> For the land, whither thou goest in to possess it, IS NOT AS THE LAND OF EGYPT, from whence ye came out, where thou sowedst thy seed, and wateredst it with thy foot, as a garden of herbs.
>
> **DEUTERONOMY 11:10**

Look at the phrase in Deuteronomy 11:10, "...**wateredst it with thy foot....** " That's talking about how difficult it was to water the seed they'd sown in the land of Egypt. They had to do it manually. They had to do it in themselves; there was no blessing on it.

Similarly, we have been watering our finances with our feet, counting on overtime, or even working two jobs, to make ends meet.

But notice Deuteronomy 8:7: "**For the Lord thy God BRINGETH thee into a good land, a land of brooks of water, of fountains and depths that spring out of valleys and hills.**" Oh, the Father so desires that His children really hear and understand His Word and take hold of it with tenacity and boldness and confidence.

But, as I mentioned before, to do that, you have to know that God wants you wealthy for a reason. He wants you to have money with a mission. Remember, He has a plan, purpose, design, and objective for you to be wealthy. Another way to say it is: *You have an assignment from God to be wealthy.*

If you are a partner with God, He wants you to have wealth. And it's not for *covetous* reasons, but for *covenant* reasons. It's not just about "me and my four and no more." It's not just about houses, lands, cars, clothes, and diamonds. No, it's about the assignment, and that assignment is to be a co-laborer with God to bring the Gospel of Jesus Christ to the nations.

Let's look again at another aspect of our golden text, Psalm 66:12.

Thou hast caused men to RIDE OVER OUR HEADS; we went through fire and through water: But thou broughtest us out into a wealthy place.
PSALM 66:12

Do you know what the revelation of the "wealthy place" can do for the Church? It can stop men in their tracks from riding over their heads.

Actually, when someone "rides over your head," he is really riding over Jesus' head, because you represent Jesus; He's Christ is *in* you (Col. 1:27). And in the area of finances, it seems that many have been laughing at the Church. They will drive by some churches and just snicker. (They don't laugh at my church, and I believe that's what God wants for every church.)

Now, don't misunderstand me. There is a fine line between arrogance and confidence or boldness. Many think I'm arrogant, but I'm not. I just know my Heavenly Father. I have discovered that He wants to bless me and that He *has* blessed me in Christ. As His child, my hand is in the "cookie jar" of His blessings, and I found out that that jar has room for many hands — for the hands of all of His children!

The 'Also' of God's Blessings

Now let's look at Psalm 105:37.

He [the Lord] **brought them** [the children of Israel] **forth also with silver and gold: and there was not one feeble person among their tribes.**

PSALM 105:37

I want you to look at the chronological order here in this verse. What did the Lord talk about first? He didn't talk about "none feeble" first; He talked about *wealthy people* first. It says, **"He brought them forth also with silver and gold...."** Then it says, **"...and there was not one feeble person among their tribes."** You can't bring people out unless you bring them out of debt.

Also, notice that God didn't just bring the children of Israel *forth*; He brought them forth *with* something.

You see, most Christians think that when they accepted Jesus Christ as their Savior, God just brought them forth from going to hell one minute to going to Heaven the next. But that's as far as they've let the Lord take them. Certainly, being saved is a part of the wealthy place, but there is more to it. There's the "also."

He brought them forth ALSO with silver and gold: and there was not one feeble person among their tribes.

PSALM 105:37

Certainly, your life in Christ is the most important thing. Spending eternity in Heaven with the Lord is more important than any earthly riches.

For God so loved the world, that he gave his only begotten Son, that whosoever believeth in him should not perish, but have everlasting life.

JOHN 3:16

Therefore if any man be in Christ, he is a new creature: old things are passed away; behold, all things are become new.

2 CORINTHIANS 5:17

But as many as received him, to them gave he power to become the sons of God, even to them that believe on his name.

JOHN 1:12

All of these scriptures have to do with being brought forth. But God wants to do more than just bring you forth. He wants to bring you forth with prosperity and health.

You remember Psalm 66:12 says, **"Thou hast caused men to ride over our heads; we went through fire and through water: but thou broughtest us OUT INTO a wealthy place."** God didn't just bring them out. He brought them *into* a wealthy place. Similarly, when you got saved, you got "brought out" of the kingdom of darkness. But God doesn't want to stop there. He wants to bring *you* into a wealthy place too!

He brought them forth also with silver and gold: and there was not one feeble person among their tribes.

PSALM 105:37

As I said, if we're born again, we have the testimony that God has brought us forth. But we've left the "also" part out. We have tried to be so spiritually deep about being brought forth that we have overlooked "also."

God didn't just turn His people loose for the world to laugh at them and shame them. No, He loosed them that the world might know that they'd been touched by Almighty God and brought forth by His strong hand! Those who saw them knew they belonged to Someone important — that they were from a very special family.

Well, what does that word "also" mean to us today? It means the same thing it meant for God's people then. **"He brought them forth also WITH SILVER AND GOLD: and there was not one feeble person among their tribes."** It means having an anointing to prosper. It means a continual supply of money coming to you. It means supernatural debt cancellation.

It sure is wonderful to be out of debt with nothing coming in but the utility bill! That's what the Lord wants to do for you. He brought you forth so He could bless you with the "also."

**FOR THE LORD THY GOD BRINGETH THEE INTO A GOOD LAND, a land of brooks of water, of fountains and depths that spring out of valleys and hills;
A land of wheat, and barley, and vines, and fig trees, and pomegranates; a land of oil olive, and honey;
A land wherein thou shalt eat bread without scarceness, THOU SHALT NOT LACK ANY THING IN IT; a land whose stones are iron, and out of whose hills thou mayest dig brass.**

> **When thou hast eaten and art full, then thou shalt
> bless the Lord thy God for the GOOD LAND which
> he hath given thee.**
>
> **DEUTERONOMY 8:7-10**

The Word of God concerning wealth really hits at
religion. Being in a land where there is no lack tears religion
up, because religion knows how to lack, and it teaches its
people how to lack! (Many are fanning themselves in
church with free funeral-home sponsored paper fans when
they should have air-conditioning. That's religion.)

Now look in Deuteronomy chapter 6, which also talks
about this "good land."

> **And it shall be, when the Lord thy God shall have
> brought thee into the land which he sware unto thy
> fathers, to Abraham, to Isaac, and to Jacob, to give
> thee great and goodly cities, which thou buildedst
> not,**
> **And houses full of all good things, which thou
> filledst not, and wells digged, which thou diggedst
> not, vineyards and olive trees, which thou plantedst
> not; when thou shalt have eaten and be full.**
>
> **DEUTERONOMY 6:10,11**

I like the first part of verse 11: **"And houses full of all
good things, which thou filledst not...."** You don't have
to try to fill your house — let Him fill it. We have been

trying to fill our houses, trying to do it in ourselves. We need to just let Him do it.

And if you don't even have a house to fill, let Him do that for you too. Let Him get you a house. He will do it. You set yourself to meditate on and be a doer of His Word. And then whatever He tells you to do specifically, do it.

Friend, there is a wealthy place in God, and He wants to take you there.

You Have a Covenant of Increase!

2

The Lord once spoke to me and said, "Tell My children that they can't dream any bigger than I can deliver." When you get hold of this revelation and begin to act on it, God will take you into your wealthy place! You will be headed for a blessing traffic jam! While you are sleeping, He will do the work — just believe Him and refuse to let go of His promise. In fact, He can increase you rapidly. It doesn't have to be a slow work. God will bring rapid increase to your house if you will take Him at His Word.

There is a promise for those who delight in God's Word.

Praise ye the Lord. Blessed is the man that feareth the Lord, that delighteth greatly in his commandments.
His seed shall be mighty upon earth: the generation of the upright shall be blessed [or empowered to prosper].
WEALTH AND RICHES shall be in his house: and his RIGHTEOUSNESS endureth for ever.
PSALM 112:1-3

Someone asked, "Yes, Brother Thompson, but what does wealth have to do with righteousness?" Look at Psalm 35:27.

Let them shout for joy, and be glad, that favour my righteous cause; yea, let them say continually, LET THE LORD BE MAGNIFIED, which hath pleasure in the prosperity of his servant.

PSALM 35:27

I tell you, the Lord is not magnified by your bills. He is magnified by your prosperity — by the prosperity that He gives. What makes the difference between the one who is prospering God's way in the land of "more than enough" and the one who is barely getting by? It's the prosperous person's willingness to magnify the Lord and His Word over his circumstances no matter how bad they may seem.

You may work a secular job with someone who's unsaved, and he's wondering how you're able to live like you're living. You're both making the same salary, but he can't keep up with you. You're always going on nice vacations and buying things he's not able to buy. Why are you so blessed? You're letting the Lord be magnified!

As I said, the Lord is not magnified by your bills. He is not magnified by your standing in line with your credit card, trembling and wondering if it will "go through" for whatever it is you want to buy.

How To Give God Pleasure With Your Life

What does the rest of Psalm 35:27 say? It says, **"...Let the Lord be magnified, WHICH HATH PLEASURE IN THE PROSPERITY OF HIS SERVANT."**

Do you want God to have pleasure in your life? Well, get rich then. Be prosperous. But let *Him* do it. Don't try to do it in yourself, gambling away what little you have on some get-rich-quick scheme. No, you do it by faith and by action — by believing God's Word and by sowing or giving.

There's a scripture that says, **"A good man leaveth an inheritance to his children's children: and the wealth of the sinner [or wicked] is laid up for the just"** (Prov. 13:22). Some people get this verse mixed up. They read, "The wealth of the wicked is laid up for the just," and think it's talking about sinners or people outside of Christ. But the word "wicked" comes from the word "wick." That's where we get our word "wicker" describing a certain kind of furniture. That word "wicked" simply means twisted. Saved people can be twisted in their thinking in certain areas, and one of those areas is money.

For example, there are "twisted" people who believe that Christians ought to be broke. They take vows of poverty. And there are some really twisted people who think the preacher ought to be *doubly* broke! They might think it's okay for a Christian to have a little something unless he's a preacher; if he's a preacher, he shouldn't have anything.

How To Speed Up Your Journey to the Wealthy Place

I tell you, God is doing something in the earth for His people in the financial arena. And I believe that now is the time He's going to speed up the wealth process. We already read Psalm 102:13, which says, **"Thou shalt arise, and have mercy upon Zion: for the time to favour her, yea, the set time, is come."**

Now look at Psalm 118.

> **This is the Lord's doing; it is marvellous in our eyes.**
> **This is the day which the Lord hath made; we will rejoice and be glad in it.**
> **Save now, I beseech thee, O Lord: O Lord, I beseech thee, send now prosperity.**
>
> **PSALM 118:23-25**

Now is the time to speed this wealth process up. Many folks are always looking to the future. They look forward to Friday when they can go out for dinner or go out for an ice cream cone. We think everything has to happen sometime in the future.

But I have a question for you? Why can't you eat ice cream on Monday? I got tired of waiting on Friday to come or the first of the month when I got paid. I thought, *Why can't I enjoy myself in the middle of the month?*

Look again at Psalm 118.

This is the Lord's doing; it is marvellous in our eyes.

PSALM 118:23

When somebody asks you how you came to be so prosperous so quickly, you can say, "This is the Lord's doing; it is marvelous in our eyes."

The Lord's Doing Doesn't Take Years To Accomplish

The God-kind of prosperity doesn't always come overnight, but it doesn't have to take years, either! Listen, friend, it is time to speed things up. If you are in debt, when do you want to be out of debt? You want to be out *now*, not years from now. You want out, and the sooner the better, right?

Then you need to declare your financial freedom right now. If you want to be out of debt now, you need to make your declaration of faith now. But it's not just a confession; you are *expecting* it now — soon, suddenly, and amazingly!

Declare *now* that all your bills are paid. Declare *now* that you are a big-time giver. Talk *now* about the Lord's doings and how marvellous they are in your eyes (Ps.

118:23). Talk *now* about His amazing grace. I tell you, faith will speed up the process.

Let me show you something else in connection with Psalm 118:23. Let's look at verse 24.

THIS IS THE DAY which the Lord hath made; we will rejoice and be glad in it.

PSALM 118:24

This is the day! Today is the day of your salvation concerning finances! You don't have to be intimidated another day about the blessings of God. You are supposed to be blessed and prosperous! You are supposed to have plenty! You are supposed to be the head and not the tail!

Save now, I beseech thee, O Lord: O Lord, I beseech thee, send NOW prosperity.

PSALM 118:25

The scripture says, "Send *now* prosperity," not tomorrow. You could say to the Lord, "I make a demand on Your power now. Send now prosperity!" Things you thought you were going to pay for in two years' time might be paid in two months. That which you thought you'd have to pay for over fifteen years could be paid in fifteen *months*! Why? Because God is sending *now* prosperity if you'll cooperate with Him!

The bank thought it was going to take me thirty years to pay off my home, but it only took me four years. I got ahold of God's Word, and He showed me how to speed it up! That house is my house and the Lord's house — free and clear.

Don't tell me things like this can't happen, because they've happened to me, and they're still happening to me! I'm too far gone, so to speak, for you to tell me that prosperity is not God's will or that His blessings have been done away with. I've been there, done that, and I'm enjoying it! I am enjoying the "promised land" — the wealthy place!

When you are not ashamed of the Gospel of Christ, and you're not afraid to take God at His Word, that is when things are going to start happening for you, and you'll be free at last without bondage, lack, or insufficiency.

Today is your day. This is the set time for victory in your finances. So make your declaration of faith, believing in your heart, and obey what God tells you to do — because you have a covenant of increase!

Laying a Foundation To Receive The God-Kind of Wealth Part 1

3

Over the years, I have met and ministered to thousands in the Body of Christ who are not prospering as they should. They tithe, they give offerings, they live morally right, they are committed to the local church, and they are submitted to spiritual authority. Yet they are broke.

There are many good Christians, even good ministers, who are broke. How can that be? There has to be a reason. Something has been hindering them. I believe the answer to that dilemma is that a proper foundation for finances has not been laid.

You see, if the tithe were the answer, we would have it — we would have prosperity. Now don't misunderstand me. Without your tithing, you are not going to be blessed. The Bible says, **"Bring ye all the tithes into the storehouse, that there may be meat in mine house, and prove me now herewith, saith the Lord of hosts, if I will not open you the windows of heaven, and pour you out a blessing, that there shall not be room enough to receive it"** (Mal. 3:10). And verse 9 of Malachi chapter 3 talks about the curse you bring upon yourself for failing to tithe.

But if the tithe were the answer, we would have it. Many have tithed for years, but have not come into the financial blessing God wanted them to have. They have not entered into the wealthy place.

I found the answer. There are a few adjustments we have to make. But when you make those adjustments, it doesn't matter what your family background or how long you've been broke, you can enter into the land of the rich!

The Lord shall command the blessing upon thee in thy storehouses, and in all that thou settest thine hand unto; and he shall bless thee in the land which the Lord thy God giveth thee
DEUTERONOMY 28:8

Notice it says, "The Lord shall command." This is a serious thing to the Lord. God wants to command His blessing. He wants to honor the covenant and see to it that His children have what belongs to them. But the blessings of God are conditional; there are things we must do to cooperate with God and His will so that He can manifest His will in our lives.

We have tried to get the blessings of God other ways — through academics, psychology, scheming, and the government. But we have failed to get wealth. If we only realized and understood that there is wealth untold that belongs to us and that we can tap in to. There is no limit to the God-kind of wealth. There are no instruments that can calibrate, no computers that can compute, and no calculators that can calculate what God can do for you! You can get to the point at which God is blessing you so much that you stop counting. That's exciting! So let's find out how to lay the proper foundation for receiving.

You Can't Build Properly Without a Good Foundation

If you were going to build a good building, the first thing you'd need to do is dig deep enough to lay a good foundation. You can't just set a building on top of anything. Once you get that foundation laid, you can build.

Similarly, one of the reasons we have not had our money is because of a bad foundation or a lack of a foundation.

What is a foundation? One definition is *natural or prepared ground or a base on which some structure rests.* Another definition is *the act of founding, setting up, or establishing footing.*

We have to establish a spiritual footing concerning money so we can build a good, solid, and strong structure of financial blessing. You know, the devil doesn't want you to enter into the wealthy place or possess any of the blessings God has provided for you. And he's going to try to stop you from walking in God's blessings. But he can't stop you; he can only try to hinder you. However, as you're meditating on God's Word and becoming intimately acquainted with your covenant rights and blessings, realize this: Satan is not going to just "roll over and play dead" and give up on trying to stop you. You are going to have to persevere in what you know.

I want to share with you nine foundational stones you'll need to lay your foundation. Look to see what's been holding you back personally and what adjustments you need to make.

Foundational Stone Number One:
Use Proven Weaponry —
The Word of God — To Fight Your Battles

When David met up with the giant Goliath, who was trying to destroy the children of Israel, David called him an uncircumcised Philistine. In other words, David knew he had a covenant with God, and David knew Goliath didn't have a covenant. (Did you know that the devil doesn't have a covenant, but you do? That gives you the definite advantage over him.)

David made up his mind that he was going to face Goliath. King Saul tried to give David his armor to wear, but David wouldn't wear it because he had not proven it.

And Saul armed David with his armour, and he put an helmet of brass upon his head; also he armed him with a coat of mail.

And David girded his sword upon his armour, and he assayed to go; for he had not proved it. And David said unto Saul, I cannot go with these; for I have not proved them. And David put them off him.

And he took his staff in his hand, and chose him five smooth stones out of the brook, and put them in a shepherd's bag which he had, even in a scrip; and his sling was in his hand: and he drew near to the Philistine.

                                                    1 SAMUEL 17:38-40

In trying to obtain finances, we've been using armor or weaponry we haven't proven. In the heat of life's battles is no time to reach for unproven weaponry.

Someone said, "But isn't the Word of God proven?" Yes, but it could be unproven in *your* life. Certainly, the Word of God is tried and true and can be depended on. But what have you been doing with the Word? Is the Word in you? Is it real to you? In other words, are God's words Spirit and life to you (John 6:63)? Can you use them in battle, or are they just words to you?

Saul had given David his armor, but David wouldn't use it because he hadn't had a chance to prove it. Instead, he went to the brook and got five smooth stones. (He really only needed one because God was in that one stone!)

We need to use proven weaponry — the Word of God hidden in our heart — when fighting life's battles, including battles in the area of finances.

Foundational Stone Number Two: Don't Be High-Minded

Now let's look at something in First Timothy 6. It is a charge to the rich, but it will help you lay a good foundation while you are in the process of getting rich. It will keep you from stumbling and falling as God prospers you more and more.

> Charge them that are rich in this world, that they be not highminded, nor trust in uncertain riches, but in the living God, who giveth us richly all things to enjoy;
> That they do good, that they be rich in good works, ready to distribute, willing to communicate;
> Laying up in store for themselves A GOOD FOUNDATION against the time to come, that they may lay hold on eternal life.
>
> **1 TIMOTHY 6:17-19**

Let's read that passage in another translation.

> Tell those rich in this world's wealth to quit being so full of themselves and so obsessed with money,

which is here today and gone tomorrow. Tell them
to go after God, who piles on all the riches we
could ever manage.
To do good, to be rich in helping others, to be
extravagantly generous.
If they do that, they'll build a treasury that will
last, gaining life that is truly life.

1 TIMOTHY 6:17-19 (*The Message Bible*)

Notice verse 17: "Tell them to go after God." That's
what you have to do — you have to go after God. I went
after Him when I was broke. Then He made me rich, and
I am still going after Him.

You're never to stop going after God. He is able to pile
prosperity upon you. He can get you to the place where
you can be extravagant in the way you live and the way
you give.

In this passage in First Timothy 6, the Apostle Paul is
giving specific commandments that apply to the wealthy.
Ephesus was a wealthy city. There were members of the
Church there who were very rich. Paul exhorted Timothy to
instruct the wealthy believer on how to handle the
prosperity God had given him.

So it's good advice for us today. Money is a powerful
force. There is a certain wisdom we have to have before we
can handle wealth, or wealth will destroy us.

Let's look at verse 17 again: **"Charge them that are rich
in this world, that they be not highminded, nor trust in**

uncertain riches, but in the living God, who giveth us richly all things to enjoy." Foundational stone number two is this: Be not high-minded.

You know, high-mindedness is not reserved for the rich. Some people are as broke as they can be, and they are high-minded. They are arrogant and offensive and display themselves as superior. They are overcome with a sense self-importance and overbearing pride.

These things ought not be, whether you are wealthy or broke!

The *New International Version* sheds some more light on First Timothy 6:17.

Command those who are rich in this present world not to be arrogant nor to put their hope in wealth, which is so uncertain, but to put their hope in God, who richly provides us with everything for our enjoyment.

1 TIMOTHY 6:17 (NIV)

You see, you have to avoid a spirit of pride, because it will try to come upon you with money. You will be tempted to become conceited and arrogant. What this verse is saying is, "Don't act ugly!" It's as simple as that.

In other words, don't stop speaking to others just because you have a nice house, a nice car, and nice clothes to wear. You have to get that straight before God will bring you into the wealthy place. You have to have a good attitude right now before you get there. Then you have to hold on to that good attitude.

God will give you the kind of house you want, the kind of car you want, and the kind of clothes you want. But you need to prove to Him you are not going to get taken with pride and arrogance and conceit.

Now let's look at Deuteronomy chapter 8 at another admonishment to be not high-minded.

All the commandments which I command thee this day shall ye observe to do, that ye may live, and multiply, and go in and possess the land which the Lord sware unto your fathers.

And thou shalt remember all the way which the Lord thy God led thee these forty years in the wilderness, TO HUMBLE THEE, and to prove thee, to know what was in thine heart, whether thou wouldest keep his commandments, or no.

And he humbled thee, and suffered thee to hunger, and fed thee with manna, which thou knewest not, neither did thy fathers know; that he might make thee know that man doth not live by bread only, but by every word that proceedeth out of the mouth of the Lord doth man live.

DEUTERONOMY 8:1-3

Verse 2 says, **"And thou shalt remember all the way which the Lord thy God led thee these forty years in the wilderness, to humble thee...."** Humble is the opposite of high-minded.

Then look at the rest of that verse: **"...AND TO PROVE THEE, to know what was in thine heart, whether thou wouldest keep his commandments, or no."** We can see from this verse why God led them through the wilderness. And the same is true for us today. In other words, one reason why some believers don't have their money yet is, they have not been proven. Their hearts are not fully turned to the Lord.

Certainly, we would *say* we would support the work of the Kingdom if we were wealthy, but the Lord knows what we will do. We may need to make an adjustment in our heart. We may need to be proven.

Let's look at a New Testament verse that talks about humility.

> **Humble yourselves therefore under the mighty hand of God, that he may exalt you in due time.**
>
> **1 PETER 5:6**

The Bible says, **"...that he may exalt you in due time."** You see, there is a due time — a due season — when the Lord knows you're ready for prosperity. Part of being ready is letting the Lord exalt and promote you and not being high-minded about it when He does. Whether or not you can be humble and remain humble is one of God's "money tests." When you can pass this test, you are well on your way to receiving divine prosperity and entering into the wealthy place.

> **For I say, through the grace given unto me, to every man that is among you, NOT TO THINK OF HIMSELF MORE HIGHLY THAN HE OUGHT TO THINK; BUT TO THINK SOBERLY, according as God hath dealt to every man the measure of faith.**
> **ROMANS 12:3**

To be a wealthy person, you have to think soberly. What is an example of humility mixed with wealth? Well, if you were a rich person, and your pastor "stepped on your toes" and said something you didn't like or made some decision you didn't approve of, would you show respect for the man and the office God has called him to? Would you submit to the pastor's authority as he is following Christ? Or would you take your money out of the church or try to start another church down the road?

Someone said, "Well, isn't that common sense? Of course, you wouldn't just take your money and run every time something didn't go your way." But some people have money, yet they have no sense to go with that money. If they had sense, they wouldn't even need the Spirit of God to convict them to make some changes.

Foundational Stone Number Three: Don't Put Your Trust in Uncertain Riches

Let's look again at First Timothy 6:17, which says, **"Charge them that are rich in this world, that they be not highminded, nor trust in uncertain riches, but in the living God, who giveth us richly all things to enjoy."** After Paul admonished the rich not to be high-minded, he said something else that we need to know in order to get our foundation laid properly. He said, **"...NOR TRUST IN UNCERTAIN RICHES, but in the living God...."**

Money is uncertain, especially money without God. You shouldn't put your trust in money because the wealth and the riches of this world are unstable. Many great fortunes have been lost overnight — people have gone to bed millionaires and have awakened broke. That's the way the world system works sometimes.

The Old Testament has something to say about trusting in uncertain riches.

> **Wilt thou set thine eyes upon that which is not? for riches certainly make themselves wings; they fly away as an eagle toward heaven.**
>
> **PROVERBS 23:5**

Now what is God saying here? He's saying, "Don't set your eyes on money. Set your eyes on Me, your source."

You can be rich, but you need to keep your eyes on God as your source.

You see, there is an anointing to prosper. You don't want money without the anointing, because that money may make itself wings and fly away! You want the anointing first and foremost. If you have the anointing to prosper, the money will come. It will always come if you know the Word and you have the proper foundation.

Some Christians are so rich in faith concerning prosperity — the anointing is on them to prosper — that it doesn't matter to them whether the money they need is in their bank account or they need to call it in by faith; it's all the same to them.

I'd rather have the anointing to prosper than to have money without the anointing. If I have money without the anointing, then if I lose the money, I'm broke, and I may never be rich again. But with the anointing, you could drop me off in a jungle somewhere with nothing but the clothes on my back, and a few months later, I'd be king of that jungle! I'd come out of there at least as one of the top men, and I'd be prosperous.

If you have the anointing to prosper, you don't worry or concern yourself with money. But if you have money without the anointing, you are going to worry about what the interest on your money is doing. You're going to be calling the bank or your broker every day to see what's happening with your money (notice I said "*your* money," because you probably wouldn't be giving God or others very much of it!). You wouldn't even be able to pray — you'd be so full of care about money.

The hope of the righteous shall be gladness: but
the expectation of the wicked shall perish.

PROVERBS 10:28

Those who put their trust in riches shall fall. Their
hope shall perish.

Trust not in oppression, and become not vain in
robbery: if riches increase, SET NOT YOUR
HEART UPON THEM.

PSALM 62:10

Set not your heart upon what? Upon increased riches!
You see, God is giving instructions to His people so He
can get a proper foundation laid in their lives and bring
them into a wealthy place. Some are already there. These
instructions are for them too. But God wants you to get
these things straight in your life before you ever get into
that land. Then when you get there, your heart won't go
astray. You'll continue to go after the things of God; you
won't let your head be turned by money.

Why did God say, "Set not your heart upon them,"
talking about riches? Because He knows that those who
put their trust in riches are going to fall.

Do you remember the rich farmer and the rich man
and Lazarus in Luke 12:16-21 and Luke 16:19-31? Both of

these wealthy men put their trust in their money instead of in God, and they fell as a result.

Money is one of the easiest things to have in your life, but you have to get ready; you have to get equipped. God will not prosper you so you can leave Him. If some people, right now, had all their bills paid and $50,000 left over, they would forget God, Jesus, and the church. They'd be out fishing on Sundays instead of going to church. It might not happen immediately, but gradually, they would forget God.

I encourage you to check up on yourself and do a spiritual inspection. Are you high-minded — conceited, arrogant, and hard to get along with? Are you trusting in what little money you do have instead of depending utterly on God? If so, you need to make an adjustment so you can lay these foundational stones and prepare yourself for receiving the wealth God has in store for you.

In review, I talked about three foundational stones for receiving wealth. They are: 1) Use proven weaponry — the Word of God — to fight your battles; 2) Don't be high-minded; and 3) Don't trust in uncertain riches.

Foundational Stone Number Four: Put Your Trust in the Living God

If we are not to put our trust in uncertain riches — riches that may be here today and gone tomorrow — in what, then, are we going to put our trust? The fourth foundational stone is closely related to the third stone, which is not putting your trust in uncertain riches. The fourth stone is this: Put your trust in the living God!

I know a few fellows who are just as humble as they can be. But if you knew what they were worth, you would faint and be shocked like the Queen of Sheba was when she went to see King Solomon. These men aren't trusting in their riches, but in the living God.

The Bible said that He, talking about Jesus, became poor that we might be rich (2 Cor. 8:9). He accomplished that for us in His death, burial, and resurrection. If Jesus hadn't risen from the grave, we might say, "Oh, isn't that nice. He became poor." But on the third day, He got up! The grave could not hold Him! Our redemption is complete, and, legally, in the mind of God, we are rich!

Instead of trusting in the wealth that God gives us, we must put our trust in God who is the source of our wealth. The Bible says, **"TRUST IN THE LORD with all thine heart; and lean not unto thine own understanding. In all thy ways acknowledge HIM, and he shall direct thy paths"** (Prov. 3:5,6).

Sometimes people trust in themselves or others to obtain wealth. But that is the same as trusting in uncertain riches. Notice the different attitudes expressed in verses 17 and 18 of Deuteronomy 8.

**And thou say in thine heart, My [own] power and
the might of mine hand hath gotten me this wealth.
But thou shalt REMEMBER THE LORD thy God:
for it is he that giveth thee power to get wealth,
that he may establish his covenant which he sware
unto thy fathers, as it is this day.**

DEUTERONOMY 8:17,18

Do you see the difference between these two verses?
Verse 17 says, "Don't say in your heart, 'My own power
and might has gotten me my wealth.'" You might say, "I
would never do that!" Yet we have tried to get wealth just
using the arm of the flesh, depending on ourselves or
others instead of on God. But when you have a covenant
and learn to tap into it, that covenant will just ease you into
prosperity — into the wealthy place.

Now look at verse 18. It says, "Remember the Lord.
He is the One who gives power to get wealth."

Your job is not your source. I'm not telling you not to
work. Your job is the place where you go to get seed.
Farmers do not live off their seed — they live off their
harvest. We are just barely existing when we try to live off
our seed. The Bible says that God gives seed to the sower
(2 Cor. 9:10), but until you become a bona fide sower, He
is not required to give you seed.

What is a bona fide sower? It is one who sows at the
Lord's command. Sowing — giving — is the key to
reaping and to entering into that wealthy place. And it

takes a certain amount of faith and trust in God to sow. In other words, you won't sow if you don't believe God is going to bless you.

You don't reap a harvest of financial blessing by marking up the pages of your Bible, underlining prosperity scriptures. And you don't reap a harvest by having prayer meetings. No, you reap a harvest of finances by trusting in the living God, and when you are trusting Him, you don't mind sowing. In fact, you are *eager* to sow because you know that is the only way you're going to reap a harvest and enter into the land of the rich.

4

Laying a Foundation To Receive The God-Kind of Wealth Part 2

In the last chapter we talked about four of the nine foundational stones that God wants in place in your life before He brings you into the wealthy place. They are: 1) Use proven weaponry — the Word of God — to fight your battles; 2) Don't be high-minded; 3) Don't put your trust in uncertain riches; and 4) Put your trust in the living God.

Now let's continue our study of laying the proper foundation to receive wealth.

Foundational Stone Number Five: Learn To Enjoy the Blessings of God

Let's read our text in First Timothy 6:17 again: **"Charge them that are rich in this world, that they be not highminded, nor trust in uncertain riches, but in the living God, WHO GIVETH US RICHLY ALL THINGS TO ENJOY."**

God wants you to enjoy life. He wants you to have good things. You have to know that God doesn't mind your having them, or you won't be diligent in receiving them. We have been taught through tradition and religion that the less you have, the more holy you are. I've come to the conclusion that the less you have, the more *unintelligent* you are, because you have a covenant with God! And God wants you *blessed*; He does not want you having *less*!

Sometimes it "cuts" when you say the word "rich" in church. The Church in general has not wanted to mess with that word. They just want to talk about Heaven and the fact that we are on our way.

Once I was preaching in a certain meeting on the subject of prosperity. I talked about having millionaire status on the inside of you, in your spirit. I was teaching the people that God wanted to bless them. Then I had one of the singers to come sing a song. He got up on the platform and starting singing about going to Heaven and what a time it will be when we get there.

Now I believe in going to Heaven! I'm going there, but not right now. And since we are on the earth right now, we need to know how to live. We can have a little bit of Heaven on earth!

That singer missed it by a hundred miles. I was preaching to the people to prompt them to receive God's blessings as reality in their lives right here on the earth, and he was telling them, "Let's go to Heaven!"

Sometimes, the only reason people talk about Heaven is, they're so dissatisfied here on earth, and they are hoping some kind of way, "God, get us out of this mess." They are not enjoying life as they should be.

But you don't have to be in a mess. You can be blessed down here. You can have days of Heaven on earth. You don't have to be burdened with bills that strap you financially.

I tell you, people are not in such a hurry to get to Heaven when they are not struggling, whether it be financially or in some other area. When you are fulfilling your part of the covenant down here, walking in the blessings of God, you are not wanting to be taken out of this realm so quickly.

In fact, if you don't fulfill your part of the covenant down here, I believe God is going to "call you on the carpet" when you do get to Heaven and show you all the things you missed that were reserved in your name — miles and miles of blessings. Why? Because if you are not walking in His blessings, you can't bless others with those blessings. You can't be a distribution center, so to speak, for God.

If God has to call you on the carpet in Heaven, you will probably say, "Oh, Lord, all that was for me?" If there's any way to hurt in Heaven, you will hurt when you see what you could have had and what you could have done for Him on the earth!

In that same prosperity meeting I was telling you about, I got to preaching, and I stepped down off the platform, getting close to the people and leaving my Bible and notepad on the pulpit. At one point, I turned around toward the pulpit, and I saw a man standing over my pad and Bible. He was sharply dressed in a beautiful brown suit with gold stripes. Now I have a personal tailor; I know what a nice suit looks like. But I have never in my life seen a suit like the one he was wearing. I looked away for a second and looked back again, and the man in the suit was gone.

Then the Lord spoke to me and said, "That was an angel of prosperity. I sent him here to back up the message that I told you to preach." Then the Lord showed me that he is not the only one; there is not just one angel of prosperity. There are groups of angels whose only assignment is to see that prosperity comes to God's people.

I was preaching in another meeting, and over the course of two days, I kept getting an impression to look over at the piano. On the third day, I got hold in my spirit what it was. No human being was sitting at that piano, but the Lord said to me, "You can't see them, but there are three angels there discussing the whole matter." And they were there every day. They were waiting for somebody to believe the message so they could help him receive it.

Hebrews 1:14 says, **"Are they not all ministering spirits, sent forth to minister for them who shall be heirs of salvation?"** talking about angels. Angels are waiting for you to take ahold of God's Word on finances, like a dog does a bone, so they can minister to you in the area of prosperity!

God wants us to enjoy life. I know that money in itself can't make you happy, but it's hard to enjoy life when you're broke.

I remember the day I took my middle son to buy him a car. His mother and I decided ahead of time what we were going to spend, but my son had his mind on something else! On the way to the dealership, he put a prosperity teaching tape in the tape player in my car. I figured he was trying to get me stirred up in my spirit and remind me that I was prosperous!

When we arrived, we were looking at hardtops, and he looked at me and said, "Dad, I really wanted such-and-such kind of convertible." Psalm 115:14 came up in my spirit, **"The Lord shall increase you more and more, you and your children."** I had to pass a money test with my own child! I asked the salesman, "Do you have what he wants?"

"Yes, Mr. Thompson," he said. "Well, clean it up for him then," I said. "He's getting it."

Then the man asked me how I was going to finance it. He had the banker ready to talk to me. I said, "When you clean it up and get it ready, my son is going to drive it home. I'm going to write you a check for it."

They got that car ready and put the top down, and my son drove off with his car. That sounds like God to me!

God wants us to enjoy His blessings. We may know God has reserved certain blessings for us, but if we never appropriate or receive them, we cannot enjoy them. We enjoy the blessings of God when they are manifested in our lives. But we will never receive them or get them manifested in our lives if we are doubting that God wants us to have them.

Wherefore be ye not unwise, but understanding what the will of the Lord is.

EPHESIANS 5:17

The Apostle Paul was admonishing believers to be wise, understanding the will of the Lord. What is the will of the Lord? We talked about it briefly in Chapter 1, but, in essence, God's *Word* is God's *will*. In other words, if we can find a blessing in the pages of His Word, we know it is His will for us to have that blessing.

The following are just some of the promises that can be found in the Word.

Beloved, I wish above all things that thou mayest prosper and be in health, even as thy soul prospereth.

3 JOHN 2

This is God's will!

The thief [Satan] cometh not, but for to steal, and to kill, and to destroy: I [Jesus] am come that they might have life, and that they might have it more abundantly.

JOHN 10:10

This is God's will!

Thou preparest a table before me in the presence of mine enemies: thou anointest my head with oil; my cup runneth over.

PSALM 23:5

This is God's will!

[The Lord] is able to do exceeding abundantly above all that we ask or think, according to the power that worketh in us.

EPHESIANS 3:20

This is God's will!

But my God shall supply all your need according to his riches in glory by Christ Jesus.

PHILIPPIANS 4:19

This is God's will!

Now let's look at First Timothy 6:17 again: **"Charge them that are rich in this world, that they be not highminded, nor trust in uncertain riches, but in the living God, who giveth us richly ALL THINGS to enjoy."**

What does that phrase "all things" include? Well, it includes being out of debt. It includes having a nice house.

I tell you, God doesn't mind your having a dream home on your mind. And He doesn't mind your *having* it — *possessing* it! God loves dreamers. You can get to the place in your faith and in your obedience to God where you will just start *thinking* about some of His blessings, and they'll show up at your front door!

I encourage you to dare to dream big for God. Dare to dream of having more. Dare to dream of giving big. Dare to dream about coming out of the status quo and about going to the top with Him!

Think about a few things you want right now. Think about where you want to live. God gives us all things richly to enjoy. As you lay a good foundation, the power of God can hit your life like never before and take you places you've never been before. The glory of God will drop down on you and put you in a position to receive like you never have before.

I dare you to believe that you can be out of debt. I dare you to believe that you can live in a dream home. I dare you to believe that you can be a big giver. God giveth us richly all things to enjoy. So learn to appropriate and enjoy the blessings of God. Others, especially religious folks, will try to intimidate you by saying, "You're just after money." But, no, they have it backwards — money is after *you*!

God said the blessing would overtake you (Deut. 28:2,15). That means it will run you down! But you have to have the Word on prosperity — the revelation of divine wealth — down in your spirit. You can't let others tell you it's not right. They will try to send you back to Egypt while God is trying to get you to the promised land!

Foundational Stone Number Six: Train Yourself To Do Good

Paul gave us more insight in First Timothy chapter 6 on preparing for prosperity.

That they DO GOOD, that they be rich in good works, ready to distribute, willing to communicate.
1 TIMOTHY 6:18

Foundational stone number six is this: Train yourself to do good. What does "to do good" mean? It means helping somebody else. The Bible says you have been called to be a blessing and that it is more blessed to give than to receive. I'd rather have the resources and be in a position to help someone else than to be lacking and needing someone else to help me.

As a Baptist boy, I never understood that it is more blessed to give, but after I got anointed and began prospering, I discovered that it is a joy to give and to do good to others. When you bless someone else, that means you have the resources to be able to do it, and that, friend, is a joy!

My wife and I recently paid off someone's house. What a joy it was to be able to do that! Before our own house was paid off, we had been paying extra on our own mortgage. Then someone came along and said, "Rev. Thompson, I'm going to pay your house off" and handed me a check and a handful of money besides.

Train yourself to do good. What you make happen for others will happen to you.

Foundational Stone Number Seven: Be Rich in Good Works

Once we've trained ourselves to do good works, we need to *continue* in our works. Galatians 6:9 says, **"And let us not be weary in well doing: for in due season we shall reap, if we faint not."** We saw in foundational stone number six that it is important to minister to the needs of other members of the Body of Christ. We need to give to the poor and to assist widows and orphans.

Proverbs 19:17 says, **"He that hath pity upon the poor lendeth unto the Lord; and that which he hath given will he pay him again."** In other words, if you are rich toward the poor, God considers it as being rich toward Him, and He will repay you. He will bless you in return and give you a harvest off your giving.

I already briefly mentioned the rich man in Luke 12 and the rich man in Luke 16, but these two men are examples of people who were not rich toward God.

Read carefully the following passages.

> **And he [Jesus] spake a parable unto them, saying, The ground of a certain rich man brought forth plentifully:**
> **And he thought within himself, saying, What shall I do, because I have no room where to bestow my fruits?**
> **And he said, This will I do: I will pull down my barns, and build greater; and there will I bestow all my fruits and my goods.**
> **And I will say to my soul, Soul, thou hast much goods laid up for many years; take thine ease, eat, drink, and be merry.**
> **But God said unto him, Thou fool, this night thy soul shall be required of thee: then whose shall those things be, which thou hast provided?**
> **So is he that LAYETH UP TREASURE FOR HIMSELF, and IS NOT RICH TOWARD GOD.**
> **LUKE 12:16-21**

There was a certain rich man, which was clothed in purple and fine linen, and fared sumptuously every day:
And there was a certain beggar named Lazarus, which was laid at his gate, full of sores,
And DESIRING TO BE FED WITH THE CRUMBS WHICH FELL FROM THE RICH MAN'S TABLE: moreover the dogs came and licked his sores.
And it came to pass, that the beggar died, and was carried by the angels into Abraham's bosom: the rich man also died, and was buried;
And in hell he lift up his eyes, being in torments, and seeth Abraham afar off, and Lazarus in his bosom.
And he cried and said, Father Abraham, have mercy on me, and send Lazarus, that he may dip the tip of his finger in water, and cool my tongue; for I am tormented in this flame.
But Abraham said, Son, remember that thou in thy lifetime receivedst thy good things, and likewise Lazarus evil things: but now he is comforted, and thou art tormented.

LUKE 16:19-25

Now this rich man didn't go to hell just because he was rich. Read verses 20 and 21 again: **"And there was a certain beggar named Lazarus, which was laid at his** gate, full of sores, And desiring to be fed with the crumbs which fell from the rich man's table: moreover the dogs came and licked his sores."

The rich man was wicked. It is implied that he didn't even help Lazarus. He was not rich toward God, because he didn't minister to the poor, and the Bible has a lot to say against that (*see* Proverbs 14:31; 17:5; 21:13; and 29:7).

You cannot enter the land of the rich — the wealthy place — if you are not rich in good works yourself.

Foundational Stone Number Eight: Be Ready To Distribute

Are you ready to distribute — to give — when the Lord tells you to? I "fall out" with excitement sometimes when He tells me to give money away. Why? Because every time God asks you to give something, He's always trying to get something better to you.

Your giving bypasses hindrances or obstacles Satan tries to put up. He is not a giver; he is a robber. So when you give in faith, you get out of his category. When you get to loving people and giving to them, you get off his turf, and he can't stop what God wants to do for you.

If you have bills you need to pay off, Jesus already knows how He is going to get you out of debt. God has a million ways to get money to you, but all He needs is one. You remember the five thousand who were fed because of the five loaves and the two fishes the little boy gave up to Jesus? (That little boy was ready to distribute!) Jesus asked Philip what they were going to do to feed all those people, but Jesus already knew what He was going to do (John 6:5,6).

Also, notice when the fish and bread were multiplied, Jesus didn't hand it out to the people Himself. He gave it to the disciples and they distributed it, because they were His "distribution center."

In the same way, God wants you to be a distribution center for Him — a pipeline that will pump out the blessings to others as He pumps them in to you.

You have to be ready to distribute. You shouldn't have to pray to get ready. If you have to pray about everything for two or three days, it could be too late for God to use you in a particular instance. Determine to be a distribution center for God.

Foundational Stone Number Nine: Be Willing To Communicate

Let's look at foundational stone number nine found in Philippians chapter 4.

Notwithstanding ye have well done, that ye did COMMUNICATE with my affliction.

Now ye Philippians know also, that in the
beginning of the gospel, when I departed from
Macedonia, no church COMMUNICATED with me
AS CONCERNING GIVING AND RECEIVING,
but ye only.
For even in Thessalonica ye sent once and again
unto my necessity.
Not because I desire a gift; but I desire fruit that
may abound to your account.
But I have all, and abound: I am full, having
received of Epaphroditus the things which were
sent from you, an odour of a sweet smell, a
sacrifice acceptable, wellpleasing to God.
But my God shall supply all your need according
to his riches in glory by Christ Jesus.

PHILIPPIANS 4:14-19

To lay a proper foundation and enter into the land of
the rich — the wealthy place — you have to give and
keep on giving; you have to "communicate as concerning
giving and receiving" (v. 15).

Notice Paul said in verse 17, **"Not because I desire a
gift: but I desire fruit that may abound to your account."**
Paul knew that the people's giving would open the door
to their receiving — to fruit abounding to their account.

In meetings, I've seen people give their last twenty or
their last hundred dollars. Your heart goes out to them,
but you can't stop them from doing it, because they're
planting. And you have to plant before you can reap.

I know too much about this business of giving and receiving to apologize for encouraging people to plant financial seed so that they can reap an abundant harvest. I can say with Paul, "No, I don't need the money; it's not that I desire a gift. But I desire that fruit may abound to the people's accounts."

In fact, I got to where I am today financially through planting — through communicating as concerning giving and receiving. Every time God told me to plant, I planted. And fruit began to abound more and more to my account.

Once fruit begins to abound more and more to your account (and it will abound when you communicate as concerning giving and receiving), you can't just stop there. You have to be willing to communicate continually. One of the greatest dangers wealthy people face is keeping riches to themselves.

There is a sore evil which I have seen under the sun, namely riches kept for the owners thereof to their hurt.

ECCLESIASTES 5:13

We have to stay in a state of readiness concerning distributing and communicating. We have to be willing. Isaiah 1:19 says, **"If ye be willing and obedient, ye shall eat the good of the land."**

So refuse to be stingy. Be willing to communicate.

Now in laying a good foundation, you need to remember that the just shall live by faith (Rom. 1:17; Gal. 3:11; Heb. 10:38). So in addition to your obedience to the Scriptures to lay a proper foundation, you need to use your faith. Once you've laid the foundation, you can make some bold confessions in faith according to the Word of God that can loose money into your life and free you to enter into the wealthy place.

A Confession

The following confession[1] is for you to say out loud, letting your heart agree.

"According to the Word of God, I declare that money cometh to the Body of Christ, and money cometh to me for the sake of the Gospel. I am laying a foundation, and God is performing His Word in my life.

"I call my local church debt-free. I call in all the necessary finances to completely pay for all the buildings, properties, and equipment, and to do everything God has called us as a church to do. We will tell the untold, reach the unreached, and help the believers walk in faith and victory by the anointed teaching and preaching of the Gospel.

"I call myself debt-free. I proclaim that I have the necessary finances to do everything God has called me to do with enough in store to bless others.

"Father, I honor You by putting You first in my finances, giving you my best in tithes and offerings. I thank You that You supply all my need according to Your riches in glory by Christ Jesus, and grant the desires of my heart. You are bringing me into my wealthy place. You are opening the windows of Heaven and pouring me out a blessing until it overflows.

"I believe I receive double in every area of my life — double anointing; double rejoicing; double in my giving; double in my receiving; double in my income; and double in my assets. I receive double in Jesus' Name.

"I call my house and all my property paid for in full. I believe I receive raises and bonus; sales and commissions; favorable settlements; estates and inheritances; interest and income; rebates and returns; discounts and dividends; checks in the mail; gifts and surprises; lost money found; bills decreased and paid off; blessings and increase.

"Thank You, Lord, for meeting all of my financial needs so that I have more than enough to give into Your Kingdom. *Money cometh to me now! You are bringing me into my wealthy place!*

---

[1]Taken from *Money Cometh!*, a confession published by Light of the World Christian Center, Topeka, Kansas.

Five Steps To Entering Your Wealthy Place

As I mentioned before, entering into the wealthy place in God does not happen overnight. There are certain steps we all must take; there are no shortcuts. But they are sure steps. In other words, if you take these steps, obeying God and His Word, you will be sure to enter in to all that He has for you!

Step One: Know and Understand That There Is a Wealthy Place in God

Many do not even know that there is a wealthy place in God. It is as if they are in a bakery shop, still crying for bread! They don't have their eyes open concerning the wealth that God has provided for them to have. Instead, they spend their lives struggling, living paycheck to paycheck. And they've been taught that that is normal.

But God does not want you so "strapped" that missing just one day of work would set you back financially for weeks! He doesn't want you so broke that you can feed and clothe your family — but only as long as nothing breaks down and needs repairing!

I tell you, it is not "normal" to be broke! And if you've been praying and confessing, but are not satisfied with the results, I encourage you to go back to the Word of God and get ahold of the fact in your spirit that there exists a wealthy place in God.

We read in Psalm 105:37, **"He [the Lord] brought them forth also with silver and gold: and there was not one feeble person among their tribes."** But some people do not know the One who did this for the children of Israel! It's as if these people are asking, "Who *is* this masked man who brings people from one place to another in their finances!" It is a mystery to them. They need a revelation.

There is a wealthy place in God, and He wants to bring you there!

I remember a time in our lives when my wife and I had no revelation in the area of finances. We were strapped financially, struggling over money, and living paycheck to paycheck. At one point, our washing machine broke, and we were too broke to get it fixed. I went into our laundry room and shut the door behind me. I said to myself, *Jesus talked to the fig tree, so I'm going to talk to this washer.* Then I said, "Lord, I love You, but You know I don't have any money." (I didn't know I was supposed to have money, and the Lord had mercy on me.)

I said, "I don't have the money to get this washing machine fixed. We've got the children's clothes to wash, and this thing has got to work." Then I laid my hands on the machine and said, "Now, washing machine, do you hear me? You are going to work until I get some money.

You are going to obey me now and start washing in Jesus'
Name!" And that machine began washing!

Now I couldn't do that now because I've prospered
greatly since that time. God has brought me into a
wealthy place, and, if I needed to, I could buy a
warehouse full of washers! But when you are on your
way to the wealthy place, talk to your stuff and command
it to obey you and work like it should!

For example, if your car is spitting and sputtering,
say, "Don't spit now. I'm not able to take you to the shop
right now. I'm headed to the wealthy place, and you are
going to work for me till I get there."

Someone might say, "I'm not talking to any car or
machine." Well, you'd *better* talk. You just might have to
do a little talking before you get there (remember, it
doesn't happen overnight). Also, remember Psalm 66:12:
**"Thou hast caused men to ride over our heads; we went
through fire and through water: but thou broughtest us
out into a wealthy place."** Sometimes men have been
"riding over our heads" so long that it takes a little while
for us to enter into the wealthy place.

In order to enter into the wealthy place, you must first
be convinced that a wealthy place exists for you in God.
You can't enter in unless you know it's real and that
wealth belongs to you.

You're probably familiar with the account of the
"prodigal son" in Luke chapter 15. This story illustrates

the fact that many do not benefit from the wealth that God has for them simply because they do not realize that it is available to them or that it belongs to them.

> And he [Jesus] said, A certain man had two sons:
> And the younger of them said to his father, Father, give me the portion of goods that falleth to me. And he divided unto them his living.
> And not many days after the younger son gathered all together, and took his journey into a far country, and there wasted his substance with riotous living.
> And when he had spent all, there arose a mighty famine in that land; and he began to be in want.
> And he went and joined himself to a citizen of that country; and he sent him into his fields to feed swine.
> And he would fain have filled his belly with the husks that the swine did eat: and no man gave unto him.
> And when he came to himself, he said, How many hired servants of my father's have bread enough and to spare, and I perish with hunger!
> I will arise and go to my father, and will say unto him, Father, I have sinned against heaven, and before thee.
>
> LUKE 15:11-18

I want you to think about this story from a different angle. You probably already know the story, and you know that the younger son who squandered his wealth eventually discovered that he messed up. He went back home, and his father forgave him, welcomed him back with open arms, and threw him a big party (Luke 15:20-24).

Now let's pick up reading at verse 25.

> **Now his elder son was in the field: and as he came and drew nigh to the house, he heard musick and dancing.**
> **And he called one of the servants, and asked what these things meant.**
> **And he said unto him, Thy brother is come; and thy father hath killed the fatted calf, because he hath received him safe and sound.**
> **And he was angry, and would not go in: therefore came his father out, and intreated him.**
>
> **LUKE 15:25-28**

Now look again at verse 28: "**And he** [the elder brother] **was ANGRY, and would not go in....**" Now when you start getting blessed, some folks are going to get angry. When I started prospering, you could just see the steam coming out of some people, even some of my family members. I mean, they were flat-footed mad at me!

When you are prospering God's way, you become a mirror of the Word, so to speak, and some people don't like looking into that mirror because it shows them that there is more that they are not walking in. They would rather see you not prospering than to turn loose of their religion, their laziness, or whatever it is that's holding them back from walking in the same blessings.

Some will hate you for prospering, because they don't want to pay the price you paid. They could have the same blessings, but they don't want to approach the Father the way the prodigal son did — in complete humility and trust. That prodigal son made an appeal to his father's mercy, and mercy is what he received.

But the elder brother wasn't very happy that the father had mercy on the younger son — on the elder son's own brother! And, sadly, that's true a lot of times in the Church today. But you will never walk in God's fullness if you have a hateful, haughty attitude toward others who are being blessed.

Look at Lot, Abraham's nephew, in the Old Testament. The Lord had called Abraham and told him that He was going to bless him and make him a blessing. The Lord didn't say anything like that to Lot that we have a record of. The Lord didn't call Lot's name. Yet we read that Lot was blessed because of his association with his uncle. We could say that Lot was "eavesdropping"!

In other words, Lot knew what the Lord had told Abraham, and Lot knew that because of what the Lord had said, Abraham was headed to a wealthy place. So he got in on it too (*see* Genesis chapters 11-13).

You see, there is a residue of anointing that can come off you and onto others when God blesses you in a certain area. And in the case of Abraham and Lot, Lot was smart enough to recognize the hand of God on Abraham and to get in on some of that anointing. But he couldn't have done that had he gotten angry with Abraham for prospering so much. No, his attitude had to have been more humble than that.

I once saw a movie in which the chauffeur who worked for an ultra-wealthy family got rich by eavesdropping. As he chauffeured this rich family from place to place, he would listen to them talk about their investments, and he would go out and do what they were doing! With what little money he had, he would invest in the same stocks and bonds they were investing in, and that chauffeur became a millionaire!

You can't despise the one who has money, or money will never come to you. You remember God said to Abraham, "I will bless you and make you a blessing. I will bless those who bless you and curse those who curse you" (Gen. 12:2,3). Similarly, you can put yourself in an unfavorable position where the blessings don't flow if you open yourself up to hating blessed, wealthy people.

Let's continue reading in Luke 15.

And he answering said to his father, Lo, these many years do I serve thee, neither transgressed

I at any time thy commandment: and yet thou
never gavest me a kid, that I might make merry
with my friends:
But as soon as this thy son was come, which hath
devoured thy living with harlots, thou hast killed
for him the fatted calf.
And he said unto him, Son, thou art ever with me,
and all that I have is thine.
It was meet that we should make merry, and be
glad: for this thy brother was dead, and is alive
again; and was lost, and is found.

LUKE 15:29-32

Some people are not prospering because they are not
living right, as in the case of the prodigal son before he
"came to himself" and repented before his father. If that
describes you, you have an invitation from Almighty God,
the Heavenly Father, to change your way of living — to
come to Him and to ask for His forgiveness. He will
forgive you and cleanse you from all unrighteousness (1
John 1:9). He will give you the best robe (Luke 15:22) and
rejoice that you've "come back home." He will bring you
out of the fire and the water of your wrong way of living
and of your financial problems and bring you into a
wealthy place.

Others are living right, but they still are not
prospering. In fact, there are a lot of Christians in the
Church who have been living right before God, but have

not prospered. Friend, living right is certainly the proper thing to do, but living right in itself will not get you into the wealthy place.

For twenty-five years, I have had no other woman in my life but my wife. I have lived right before my children. There was never a time when their mother had to tell them she didn't know where I was. I preached on Sunday mornings, and on Saturday nights, I was at home with my family. I kept my family in church. I didn't curse, and I didn't cheat others. I tried to help everyone I could. Yet I was broke.

Years ago, I went to a certain prayer meeting and got on my face before God and said, "I've been on the King's Highway a long time, but there's one thing I need to know. Where is my money? Where is my silver and gold? Where is my portion of the earth and the fullness thereof that the Word says belongs to You [1 Cor. 10:26]? I'm part of Your family — where's my stuff!"

You see, just being in the family won't necessarily get you into the wealthy place. Divine wealth belongs to you if you're in the family, but you have to appropriate it by faith for it to become a reality in your life so that you can actually enjoy it.

The righteous have a wealthy place in God. They have certain rights. But if they are not enjoying them, it's not the Father's fault.

Notice the elder son's attitude when the father made a fuss over his younger son, and notice how the father answered the elder son.

And he [the elder son] **answering said to his father, Lo, these many years do I serve thee, neither transgressed I at any time thy commandment: and yet thou never gavest me a kid, that I might make merry with my friends....**
And he said unto him, Son, THOU ART EVER WITH ME, and ALL THAT I HAVE IS THINE.

LUKE 15:29,31

Can you hear the Heavenly Father speaking to you in this verse? All that He has is yours, but why you don't have it is not His fault. However, God is a good and gracious Heavenly Father, and He will help you get it if you will humble yourself and do what He says to do.

Notice in verse 31 what the father was saying to his elder son. He was saying, "Hey, son, you can kill a calf when you get ready. You are my son; you can go and kill a whole herd if you want to! It doesn't matter to me. Knock yourself out — call all your friends over!"

Apparently, this son didn't realize his rights and privileges as a son in his father's house. That is where the Church has been. We have not known that the Father wants us to be fully supplied.

The father in Luke 15 said to the elder son, "Everything I have belongs to you." Similarly, God the Father is saying to you, "Everything I have belongs to you."

The righteous have a wealthy place in God. But if they are too stubborn or rebellious to change, they won't enter in. Some people just don't want to change. They don't want to change their thinking. But to enter into the wealthy place, you have to be willing and humble enough to change. You have to be willing to look at the Word like you've never looked at it before. You have to be willing to change the company you keep if need be. For example, if you are hanging around negative, broke people who talk poverty, you need to find some new company. You can't run with poverty-minded folks and be wealthy. You can love them, but you don't have to develop close friendships with them.

I'm talking about the wealthy place that exists for you in God. I can't tell you how to get there until I convince you that it exists and that it belongs to you. If you don't know and accept the fact that there is a wealthy place reserved for you, you aren't going to go there.

But you belong there! I am living there in that wealthy place. I've spied out the land, so to speak, and I'm telling you it's a wonderful place — a place where you have no bills, a fat checking account, and the ability to give to men and women of God as the Father directs.

Step Two: Locate Wealth

What is the wealthy place that God wants to bring you into? It's in the land of "more than enough." But before I talk about that land, I have to talk about two other lands where too many Christians have been living.

The Land of 'Not Enough'

The Lord once spoke to me about this land, saying, "There are many who justify their being in this land." In other words, they come up with some kind of justification or excuse for being broke, such as, "Not everyone is supposed to be rich," and they try to "explain away" why they don't have money.

Or they'll say, "I don't want much. I just love the Lord. I pray and read my Bible. I don't need material things." That is religious thinking, and the devil will help folks come up with excuses like this all day long. He will give you plenty of ideas as to why you shouldn't have money so that you can justify your poverty.

This is the land where many live or have lived at one time or another. It is a land of struggling and never having enough, and it is a land of distress and bondage.

Then thine heart be lifted up, and thou forget the Lord thy God, which brought thee forth out of THE

LAND OF EGYPT, from THE HOUSE OF BONDAGE.

DEUTERONOMY 8:14

The last part of this verse gives a description of the land of "not enough." It says, "**...from the house of bondage.**" You see, in the land of "not enough," there is bondage. There is no freedom.

God talked about the land of Egypt as being "the house of bondage." Egypt is a type of the world, and even though the child of God has been saved, he can still be in the category of being in financial bondage. He could still be broke, or he could be in the land of "just enough," going from one financial crisis to another.

God wants us to become so dependent upon Him and so confident of the covenant that whether the economic system is stable or in a crisis, we are prosperous, not broke and barely getting by. Why? Because our economic status is not determined by the world system, but by the Word of God.

If you knew there was both a financial crisis and a financial outpouring coming, which one would you want to be in? You'd want to be in the arena of the financial outpouring, wouldn't you? Well, you can, but you have to allow God to get you there.

The Land of 'Just Enough'

Just about everybody parks here in the land of "just enough." They aren't trying to justify why they're here; they are satisfied with being here. They have just enough and are barely getting by. But they are satisfied. And you know that if you're satisfied, you're not going to fight. You won't fight for your rights or try to have more.

This land is a land of having just enough to make ends meet — of having just enough to pay all your bills and buy some ice cream and a hamburger with what's left over. But having just enough is not good enough. Yet some people camp in this land. They are satisfied with scraping by. Their basic needs are met, and they think they've arrived. In fact, if they have two cars and a carport, they think they're having Heaven on earth. And don't let them get a garage with an automatic door opener — then they'll really think they're somebody!

You don't often hear of someone going from the land of "not enough" to the land of "more than enough" without spending some time in the land of "just enough." Why does God bring us up "one land at a time"? He does it so we can learn our lessons.

And thou shalt remember all the way which the Lord thy God led thee these forty years in the wilderness, to humble thee, and to prove thee, to

**know what was in thine heart, whether thou
wouldest keep his commandment, or no.
And he humbled thee, and suffered thee to hunger,
and fed thee with manna, which thou knewest not,
neither did thy fathers know; that he might make
thee know that man doth not live by bread only,
but by every word that proceedeth out of the
mouth of the Lord doth man live.**

DEUTERONOMY 8:2,3

Now you probably know what the manna scenario
was. God brought His people bread, but they were not
allowed to have leftovers. They had to gather just enough
each day. There were some who tried to gather extra, and
it rotted and became infested with worms. Why? Because
God had brought them into the land of "just enough." He
brought them bread, but they were not permitted to keep
any over and above what they needed for that day; they
were only to gather "just enough." (*See* Exodus 16:1-31.)

When God brought the children of Israel into the
wilderness — into the land of "just enough" — He
wanted them to understand that man does not live by
bread alone, but by every word that proceeds from the
mouth of God (Deut. 8:3). You see, in every land you're
in, you have to learn your lesson.

Do you want to go to the wealthy place where you're
out of debt and able to give big? Then you have to learn
your lessons. In the land of "not enough," you have to

learn to utterly depend on God. Then when you get to the next land — the land of "just enough" — you have to learn that you need to *continue* to depend on Him, because He is your source. You can't get cocky just because your bills are paid.

Did you know that if you are living on credit, you are living in the land of "not enough"? The Lord once spoke to me, saying, "Tell My children that if they are living on credit, they are living on welfare compared to the land that I have prepared for them."

Someone said, "Well, I use credit cards, but I pay the minimum that's due each month, so I'm not really in debt." Well, on some of those cards, you could run up a certain balance, pay the credit card company $20 a month, and *never* finish paying on that thing!

Some people don't like to hear someone talk to them about their credit cards. But if they are keeping a balance on a credit card month after month, with no end in sight as to when they can pay it off in full, they need to be shocked to their spiritual senses. They need to realize where they're at and understand that they're not doing as well as they thought they were. They are not where God wants them to be.

I always encourage people who are in the land of "not enough" not to be condemned, but to believe God to pay off their bills. (You have to start somewhere.) Then they can go on to the land of "just enough" and, finally, on to the land of "more than enough."

The Land of 'More Than Enough'!

This is the land we're headed to! Why is it so important to get to this land — to the wealthy place? Because when you have more than enough, you can help your neighbor. This is part of knowing and fulfilling your covenant. As I already said, God told Abraham, talking about the covenant He was making with His man Abraham, "...**I will bless thee...and thou shalt be a blessing**" (Gen. 12:2). In other words, God told Abraham, "I will bless you and your family so much that you will have to give some of your blessings away."

When you are blessed like God wants you to be blessed, you will have to find somebody to give something to!

What land are you in today? Many want others to believe they are in some land that they're really not in. They have what I call a "false prosperity." They have fancy purses, but the true test is what's in the purse — tissues or money!

Some Christians have scriptures written on their checks, but those checks are bouncing all over the place, hitting every wall! You can't even catch those checks — they're bouncing and running all over the place! That's not where God wants you to be.

If you're not in the land of "more than enough," know that God wants to take you there. God said to me, "When My children walk in My wealth, I am being glorified."

I am actually living in that land. I give God all the glory and praise and honor for bringing me into the land of "more than enough." I am living proof that you can go to the wealthy place. I have spied out the land, and my job is to come back and tell you that, yes, there are giants in this land (*see* Numbers 13:17-29), but God has given every one of His children a slingshot to kill their Goliath!

I am writing this book to encourage you that you can go to the wealthy place. It doesn't matter what your condition, your situation, or your occupation. If you are a janitor at a corner store, if you are a child of God, you can go to the land of "more than enough"!

Step Three:
Be Willing To Encounter Obstacles — Giants — And Withstand Them With the Word of God

Know this: Many will not go into the wealthy place in God because of the giants. What do I mean by "giants"? I'm talking about obstacles and hindrances that will try to keep you from even *thinking* about a wealthy place.

Let's look at an Old Testament example of the giants that stood between God's people and their Promised Land.

And they [the twelve spies] **told him** [Moses], **and
said, We came unto the land whither thou sentest
us, and surely it floweth with milk and honey;
and this is the fruit of it.
28 NEVERTHELESS the people be strong that
dwell in the land, and the cities are walled, and
very great: and moreover we saw the children of
Anak there.**

NUMBERS 13:27,28

God's people had searched the land. Sure enough, it
was a prosperous land just as God had said. And God
had said it was theirs; it belonged to them. But because
they saw giants there, they chose not to take God at His
Word and enter in to possess the land that He'd given
them.

Doesn't that sound like many in the Body of Christ
today? What are some of the giants we face that try to
hinder our prosperity? One giant is what I call a
"broke" mentality: "Well, I've been broke all of my
life. My daddy was broke, and his daddy before him
was broke. We are a broke family." But it doesn't
matter how long you've been broke, what your last
name is, or what side of the tracks you live on —
there is a wealthy place for you in God. Will you let
Him take you there?

Faith Is 'Now'

In Numbers 13:30, Caleb said, "...Let us go up at once, and possess it; for we are well able to overcome it."

Now Caleb saw the same giants the other spies saw. In effect, Caleb said, "I saw the Amalekites, the Hittites, the Jebusites, the Amorites, the Canaanites, and all the other '-ites,' but God told us it belongs to us, so let's take it!"

Also notice that Caleb didn't say, "Let's go *tomorrow* and take it." No, he said, "Let us go *at once* and take it." Faith is now; it's not tomorrow or next week. Faith says, "I see it in the Word. It's mine; I have it now."

Let's continue reading in Numbers 13.

And there we saw the giants, the sons of Anak, which come of the giants: and we were in our OWN SIGHT as grasshoppers, and so we were in THEIR SIGHT.

NUMBERS 13:33

Do you know what kind of sight they're talking about here? They're talking about sight without the Word. You have to see yourself wealthy according to the Word, not according to your last name, where you are from, or even according to your own earning power.

They said, **"...we were IN OUR OWN SIGHT as grasshoppers...."** What makes a Christian stalwart? Being full of the Word and the Spirit. You see, if you read and meditate on the Word and pray in tongues, you won't be a grasshopper. You'll be strong, and you'll possess or appropriate that which belongs to you in Christ, including divine prosperity.

Step Four: Expand Your Capacity To Receive Wealth

If you want God to bring you into a wealthy place, you're going to have to cooperate with Him by expanding your capacity to receive wealth. Notice in Numbers 13, which we just read, that most of the spies were afraid of the giants. But Caleb and Joshua had a different spirit about them. They said, "Let us go right now and take our land!"

And Caleb stilled the people before Moses, and said, LET US GO UP AT ONCE, AND POSSESS IT; FOR WE ARE WELL ABLE TO OVERCOME IT.
But the men that went up with him said, We be not able to go up against the people; for they are stronger than we.
And they brought up an evil report of the land which they had searched unto the children of Israel, saying, The land, through which we have gone to search it, is a land that eateth up the inhabitants thereof; and all the people that we saw in it are men of a great stature.

And there we saw the giants, the sons of Anak, which come of the giants: and we were in our own sight as grasshoppers, and so we were in their sight.

NUMBERS 13:30-33

The men who felt like grasshoppers in their own sight and in the sight of their enemies refused to take a step forward in faith and obedience to the Lord, and it cost them. They didn't enter in to what God had for them because they had no capacity to receive wealth.

Some way or another, if you are going to receive in life what God has for you, you are going to have to be willing to take a step forward in faith from the mess you're in, toward the promise of God. When you do, God will meet you there. If your faith is really in God and His Word, your faith will not be denied — not now, not ever!

Number Five: Take the Limits Off God!

I want you to notice something about the children of Israel's deliverance from Egypt and their journey to the Promised Land.

Yea, they TURNED BACK and TEMPTED GOD, and LIMITED THE HOLY ONE OF ISRAEL.

PSALM 78:41

The children of Israel tempted the Lord by turning back. They limited what He could do for them.

How To Tempt God and Stay
Out of Your Wealthy Place

You know, just because the Bible promises you something or just because God wants to do something for you doesn't mean it's just going to happen without any effort or cooperation on your part. Some people will say, "Well, if God wants me to have such-and-such, He'll just give it to me. He'll just do it."

The following verse talks indirectly about the part we have to play in God's bringing us into our wealthy place. This verse tells us what *not* to do if we want God to prosper us!

> **Yea, they turned back and tempted God, and LIMITED the Holy One of Israel.**
>
> **PSALM 78:41**

For God to bring you into your wealthy place, you are going to have to take the limits off Him in your life. You are going to have to stop judging God according to the White House, the Governor's Mansion, or the ultra-wealthy who live in palaces.

What do I mean by that? You're going to have to stop seeing certain people as "big-timers" compared to little ol' you and poor ol' God. The wealthiest of the wealthy on this earth can't touch God. They are not really big-timers compared to Him.

Psalm 78:41 is a pivotal verse to understanding how *not* to enter into the wealthy place! What you do with this verse will determine whether or not you enter into divine prosperity.

Don't you do what the children of Israel did in tempting and doubting God and limiting His power and His ability in their lives. Determine that you are not going to turn back this time. Determine that you are not going to tempt God through doubt and unbelief and that you are not going to let yourself be talked out of His blessings. Don't be intimidated by the world, telling you how much you can and cannot have. Start living a Word-oriented life. I have a saying, "There is nothing I can't have; there is nowhere I can't go." In fact, you should take the word "can't" out of your vocabulary.

The children of Israel limited God. How did they limit Him? By doubting Him and His Word to them. They let circumstances dominate them. God had said, "The land is yours," but the giants living in the land were more real to them than God's Word. Those giants had a higher place in their lives than the Word of God.

Someone said, "Yes, but how does that apply to me?" Don't you know that you can limit God in your own life? You can limit Him and His power in your life by your natural thinking. For example, the state of the economy can become more real to you than the Word of God.

Just take all the limits off God and begin to look at Him as the God who is able to do anything that He said He would do. Then learn how to cooperate with Him so He can do it for you.

After You've Taken the Limits Off God, Adjust Your Vision

Some of our biggest problems are the limits we've placed on God in our lives. There are some places where God wanted to bring us financially, but He couldn't, because we couldn't handle it. We couldn't think that high, and we couldn't believe it. We couldn't even adjust to seeing ourselves having that much; it made us uneasy. God has wanted to give us some nice things, but we have thought we weren't good enough for them, and we've backed off. We've said, "God, give us this little bit, and we'll be happy."

My prayer is, "God, give the little bit to the person who wants it, but, God, I want You to be big in my life!" You see, God can't bring you into your wealthy place as long as you are limiting Him.

Some believers limit God by looking at their family members who are struggling financially. They think, *Cousin So-and-so doesn't have anything. What makes me think I'm going to get it?* Well, if your cousin isn't Bible-taught, he isn't going to the wealthy place. But you can, so stop looking at your family members. You're limiting God when you do.

Other Christians limit God by looking just to their job as their source of income. All they can think is putting in overtime or taking on another job to get prosperity. But your job income is not enough to satisfy the measure of what God wants for you. You must take the limits off God in order for Him to bring you into a wealthy place.

Let me show you a favorite verse of mine that is what I call a "limit-breaker."

Now unto him that is able to do EXCEEDING ABUNDANTLY ABOVE all that we ask or think, according to the power that worketh in us.
                                            EPHESIANS 3:20

I like those words "exceeding abundantly above"! This is what God wants to do for you. But it will only happen "according to the power that worketh in you," not according to your job or your own strength or ability.

We have been trying to get there ourselves. We have been tithing, giving offerings, going to special meetings, and sending checks to television ministries. We have read books on finances, confessed till our throats were dry, and we've gotten ourselves a glass of water and confessed some more! Still the manifestation has not shown up for good people of God who really love Him and should already be in their wealthy place because of their love for God.

Now I'm not saying that the things we've been doing are not important. Certainly, we should tithe and give offerings. We should attend meetings and support television outreaches. We should read good Word-based books on prosperity, listen to good teaching tapes, and watch good videos. And we should certainly confess the Word of God. We should do all these things to plow through religious teaching and doubt and unbelief. Many around us will try to tell us that prosperity is not God's will. But the Bible says that it is.

So we should do all the good things I mentioned previously — tithe, give, and so forth. But we can't just do them to be doing them. We can't just go through the motions. What we do has to mean something. We have to have a revelation of God's will in the area of prosperity. Then we'll be able to tap into God's resources as He brings us into a wealthy place.

We do not want to do what the children of Israel did in turning back and tempting God. We need to have the attitude about the deliverance that Christ purchased for us, we are not turning back this time!

How are you limiting God in your life today? You may need to forget you even have a last name. Don't associate the wealthy place in God with your family background or history. Doing so will only hold you back.

You might even have to distance yourself from certain family members who will drag you down with poverty talk, negativism, and every other kind of "-ism" you can think of. They could keep you out of your wealthy place if you continue to listen to them.

Reverse This Verse!

We need to respect Psalm 78:41, but we need to reverse this verse in our lives! In other words, we need to learn from the example of these Old Testament saints and refuse to be turned back by man, religion, the world system, or our own unbelief.

Instead, we need to determine to live Word-oriented lives. We need to have the attitude, *I refuse to be broke. I refuse lack to come anywhere near my house, my family, my job, or any area of my life. There is nothing I can't have. There is no place I can't go.*

As I said, take certain words, such as "can't" and "lack," out of your vocabulary. As you do, you will begin to take the limits off God in terms of what He can do in your life.

Natural thinking limits God. Putting your eyes on the world's economical system hinders Him from working in your life according to His Word — according to His supernatural power. But looking at God as the God who can do anything will permit Him to work on your behalf.

So I encourage you to take your eyes off your own natural power and put them on His supernatural power to prosper you and bring you into that wealthy place!

6

The Wealthy Place Is Reserved for the Obedient

The blessings of God, including divine prosperity, are conditional. In other words, God promises them, and He stands behind His Word to make them good in our life, but we have a part to play too. The blessings won't just fall on us. We have to cooperate with God according to His Word. We have to walk in faith and in obedience. We must meet the conditions.

All of God's blessings that He promised to the children of Israel were based upon their obedience, and the same is true for us today. Obedience is a key ingredient to obtaining wealth.

> **If ye be willing and obedient, ye shall eat the good of the land:**
> **But if ye refuse and rebel, ye shall be devoured with the sword: for the mouth of the Lord hath spoken it.**
>
> **ISAIAH 1:19,20**

You have to "strain" sometimes in walking in faith and obedience — in doing some things that the flesh doesn't want to do. You have to strain when your neighbor, your fellow church member, and even your family members are not walking in faith and obedience.

You have to have the attitude, *I'm going to stick with this, no matter what!*

Well, it takes effort to do that. You could compare it to the physical training of prize-winning athletes. The only way they are going to win and keep on winning is through determination, diligence, and discipline. They have to keep running when they want to stop. They have to strain and push themselves harder and harder. They can't settle for the status quo.

It's time for the Church to exercise this kind of determination. Christians need to learn to put their flesh under and not give in to every thought and feeling that comes along that exalts itself against the knowledge of God's Word (2 Cor. 10:5).

Let's read two more verses that connect obedience to God's blessings.

If they obey and serve him, they shall spend their days in prosperity, and their years in pleasures. But if they obey not, they shall perish by the sword, and they shall die without knowledge.

JOB 36:11,12

You don't need any interpretation here. Obedience is the key to wealth. I'm telling you, the reason I am where I am in my ministry and in my personal life is, my wife and I obeyed God. We obeyed Him in our finances and in every area. You cannot violate spiritual laws and still expect, in faith and confidence, the blessings of God.

But your obedience is a choice. God will not force you to obey Him as if you were some kind of robot. You can curse at and talk about the preacher, or you can be humble and teachable.

What do I mean by teachable? Well, if a man or woman of God says something that goes cross-grain to what you believe, at least put it on a shelf, so to speak. Get out your Bible and study the subject to see whether it be so. Be like the Bereans Luke talked about in the Book of Acts: *"These were more noble than those in Thessalonica, in that they received the word with all readiness of mind, and searched the scriptures daily, whether those things were so"* (Acts 17:11).

We know that, in the Old Testament, if the Israelites were obedient to God, they lived under an open Heaven and received His blessings. The following verse describes what happened when the children of Israel obeyed God and did what He told them to do.

For the land, whither thou goest in to possess it, is NOT as the land of Egypt, from whence ye came out, where thou sowedst thy seed, and WATEREDST IT WITH THY FOOT, as a garden of herbs.

DEUTERONOMY 11:10

I touched on this briefly in another chapter, but in this verse, God was reminding His people that things were hard in Egypt. And it's hard in your "Egypt" too! It's hard paying all those bills and having nothing left over. It's hard having more bills than you have money. It's hard having creditors sending you letters and calling your house, getting smart with you.

What does that phrase mean, "wateredst it with thy foot"? That's talking about doing things in your own power or might to try to make something happen. And that's a hard road to travel; it can be wearisome. That's what the children of Israel experienced in Egypt. There was no anointing to prosper there. They toiled hard in the flesh to get what little bit they had.

Often, people "water with the foot" today when both the husband and wife have to work just to make ends meet. And, many times, the husband has two jobs or works so much overtime, his family never sees him.

Another example of watering with the foot is scraping by at the stores, always looking for sales and deals, and cutting coupons to try to save a dollar or two. I once had a cashier at a local grocery store ask me if I had a certain kind of savings card. I said, "No, I have a green card — it's called cash. Just let me pay for my stuff. I want to get out of here!"

I don't need charity. Some people look for charity when they're not really broke. They don't need charity. They have a little money (and some of them have a lot of money), but they're still looking for a deal and a handout. I read a book one time about how some everyday folks become millionaires. They do it by never spending money. They hoard money and rob themselves of life's blessings. They scrape by, robbing their children and their grandchildren. Instead of buying them nice things for Christmas, they look for sales and buy cheap stuff.

When I read that book, I decided that I didn't want to be a millionaire like that. I want to buy the good stuff and still have money. (Buying the good stuff broke and on credit isn't real prosperity, either.)

God said, **"For the land, whither thou goest in to possess it, is not as the land of Egypt, from whence ye came out. . . "** (Deut. 11:10) You see, God was trying to get them to look to the wealthy place. They wanted to go back to Egypt and "water with the foot," forfeiting God's blessing — just because they were having a little bit of a hard time! But God was trying to tell them that nothing they were experiencing was harder than what they'd come out of.

The enemy tries to discourage God's people today. He tries to slap some test or trial on them to make them back off from the truth. But you need to look him in the eye and say, "I know who you are, and I know what you're doing. I bind you in the Name of Jesus. I'm headed for the wealthy place, and you are not going to stop me."

I found out from the Word of God that I have authority over Satan and that he can't hurt me (Luke 10:19)!

Let's continue reading in Deuteronomy 11.

> But the land, whither ye go to possess it, is a land of hills and valleys, and drinketh water of the rain of heaven:
> A land which the Lord thy God careth for: the eyes of the Lord thy God are always upon it, from the beginning of the year even unto the end of the year.
> And it shall come to pass, if ye shall hearken diligently unto my commandments which I command you this day, to love the Lord your God, and to serve him with all your heart and with all your soul,
> That I will give you the rain of your land in his due season, the first rain and the latter rain, that thou mayest gather in thy corn, and thy wine, and thine oil.
>
> **DEUTERONOMY 11:11-14**

First, God told the Israelites that the land He had given them to possess was not like the land of Egypt where they'd come from. It wasn't a land of slavery, bondage, poverty, and lack.

Then God describes the Promised Land to them in verses 11 through 14. Notice verse 12: **"A land which the Lord thy God careth for: the eyes of the Lord thy God are always upon it, from the beginning of the year even unto the end of the year."**

Can you imagine having the Lord care for your financial situation? Can you imagine Him continually watching your finances — your purse or wallet, your checking account, your savings account, and your investments — all year long?

Now notice verse 14: **"That I will give you the rain of your land in his DUE SEASON, the first rain and the latter rain, that thou mayest gather in thy corn, and thy wine, and thine oil."**

Certainly, faith is now, and we are to expect from God's Word right now — today. But there is also a due season in which those things you have been standing for begin coming to pass. And don't misunderstand me. Yes, God wants us to possess divine prosperity and enter into the wealthy place. But it is not just so you can have more houses, cars, diamonds, and clothes. No, divine prosperity is so you can help set the captive free with your finances. It costs money to put the Gospel on TV, on the radio, and in print. The eternal destiny of many is in our pockets!

I said before that the blessings the Israelites received hinged on their obedience. If they were obedient, they lived under an open Heaven. However, if they were disobedient, they lived under a closed Heaven; they were cursed.

Deuteronomy 18:1-14 lists the blessings that would come upon the children of Israel if they were obedient and diligent in hearkening unto the Lord's Word or commandments.

Then Moses told them what would happen if they were *not* obedient.

> But it shall come to pass, if thou wilt NOT hearken unto the voice of the Lord thy God, to observe to do all his commandments and his statutes which I command thee this day; that all these curses shall come upon thee, and overtake thee.
>
> DEUTERONOMY 28:15

This passage in Deuteronomy 28 talks about the blessings of obedience and the curses of disobedience. Notice there is no neutral ground. In other words, you will either take the blessings, or the curses will overtake you. (Also, did you notice that the curses for disobedience seem automatic, but the blessings have to be activated and appropriated by faith?)

Your Obedience Will Prompt 'Acts of Honor'

Many do not associate honor with obedience, but the two are very closely connected. It's very simple: Your obedience honors God, and your *dis*obedience *dis*honors Him.

**HONOUR the Lord with thy substance, and with
the firstfruits of all thine increase:
So shall thy barns be filled with plenty, and thy
presses shall burst out with new wine.**

PROVERBS 3:9,10

I don't know anybody who wouldn't want what verse
10 is talking about — barns filled with plenty and presses
bursting out with new wine. In our modern day, we could
just say it's talking about abundance! Well, to get the
blessing of verse 10, you are going to have to be obedient
to verse 9, which says, **"HONOUR THE LORD with thy
substance, and with the firstfruits of all thine increase."**

Giving of your substance and your increase is a
means of honoring God as the source of your blessings.
When you honor God as the source of your blessings, He
becomes a "blesser" to you. You give the Lord an avenue
whereby He can do for you what He's always wanted to
do. You bypass Satan's dictates, because God has a legal
right to bless you when you honor Him.

Matthew 18:18 says, **". . . Whatsoever ye shall bind
on earth shall be bound in heaven: and whatsoever ye
shall loose on earth shall be loosed in heaven."** In other
words, God is saying, "Whatsoever you bind on earth, I'll
bind in Heaven. Whatsoever you loose on earth, I'll loose
in Heaven." When you begin to loose your money to
God, God has a right to loose money unto you.[1]

As long as Israel was faithful in paying their tithes and giving offerings, they prospered. But when they forgot about God, withholding from Him, they reaped the curses.

Honoring God with our substance by paying our tithes and giving offerings opens the door for us to receive supernatural provision. *Dis*honoring Him by withholding our substance closes that door and causes us to miss His promised blessings. The choice is ours. Which will we do?

I encourage you to take a personal inventory. Are you honoring God with the very best of your substance, recognizing Him as your source of supernatural provision?

I said previously that now is the Church's set time of God's favor to receive divine prosperity and enter into the wealthy place. There is a financial anointing on the Body of Christ, and those who cooperate with that anointing and yield to it in faith and obedience will cause that anointing to be released upon them in a greater measure. The anointing is present. God is ready. All you have to do is follow His orders, and the Lord will make you abound in prosperity.

God did not plan for you to barely survive or to struggle and worry about how you will pay your bills or how you will make it from one paycheck to another. That is not God's plan. He did not plan for your family to suffer from lack of food or clothing or the other necessities of life. His plan for you is abundance. He has made a way for you to have it. So why not follow His plan?

The key to releasing God's blessings into your life is dependent upon two things: 1) your act of faith; and 2) your obedience to God. You have to do more than just claim and confess. You have to have a revelation of God's Word in your heart, and you have to act as if it is true, because it is. Then you have to obey Him — His Word and His specific will for your life. In other words, when He tells you to do something, you do it.

You have to follow the laws of the Spirit in order to be a participant and a partaker in the things of God and receive of the blessings of the Spirit. The wealthy place is reserved for the obedient. Once you are obedient, you can exercise faith to appropriate the financial blessings God has in store for you.

A Confession

The following is another confession I encourage you to say out loud, letting your heart agree.

"I confess in the Name of Jesus that I am living in the perfect will of God. I desire to do the will of God, and I know that God's will for me is abundance. The will of God is that I have more than enough. I have a covenant with God. I am in partnership with Him. The anointing for prosperity has been released upon me through my faith and obedience. I have found out God's Word on the matter. I am in agreement with the Word, and, as the Word says, so shall it be in my life.

"I am willing and obedient, and the Bible says that if I am willing and obedient, I shall eat the good of the land. I am prospering in my spirit, in my soul, in my body, and in my finances. I am trusting in the Lord, and I will not go down for one split second. I honor God with my substance, and my 'cup runneth over' with blessings. From this day forward, I am free from financial bondage. I am entering into the wealthy place!"

---

[1]For an in-depth study on the subject, *see* Dr. Leroy Thompson's book *Money, Thou Art Loosed!*

A Financial Breakthrough Awaits You!

7

On the other side of your doing what God's Word has told you to do concerning finances, a financial breakthrough awaits you. I touched on it briefly in the last chapter, but there is a principle of honoring God with your income that will bring increase to your life like nothing else will. In fact, if you *don't* honor God with your income — by giving offerings — you will not prosper God's way and enter into the land of the rich.

There are two basic criteria for walking in divine prosperity: 1) *know and understand that it is indeed God's will that you prosper*; and 2) *appropriate prosperity by faith*.

We talked about God's willingness to prosper His children. Now let me explain appropriating prosperity by faith. There is a lot more to faith than just confessing something positive or even confessing the Word. For example, we learned in the last chapter that obedience works together with faith. You have to be willing and obedient to do all of the Word of God, not just the "name-it-and-claim-it" part.

The problem is, we've heard so many messages on money, but we've only been getting a little bit of information here and there. We need to get in on the full flow.

Faith demands works. James chapter 2 says that faith without works is dead (vv. 20,26). But works alone won't cut it if there's no faith behind those works. For example, sometimes the Holy Spirit moves on a congregation to just spontaneously come to the altar to lay their offerings on the platform. No one directs them to do it; they are inspired to do it. There is a special anointing for giving at that moment. Yielding to the Spirit and getting in on the flow opens the door for God to bless them in a big way if they'll expect big.

But, on the other hand, just going to the altar doesn't mean you're going to get anything. You could be going to the altar just to be going or because others are going, and it won't do you any good. No, you have to mix faith with your actions, or they are just actions. You're just going through the motions, and no heavenly reward or blessing will come out of doing that.

So we know that simply claiming God's promises of prosperity is not enough to give you a financial breakthrough. First, you have to be convinced — fully persuaded — of the will of God concerning prosperity. Then you have to appropriate financial prosperity by *faith*, and that "by-faith" clause is talking about living a *lifestyle* of faith. In other words, the Lord wants to see in your words and actions that you believe *everything* you read in His Word, not just a few "pet" verses.

For example, we know that we have to be obedient in our giving if we want to reap a financial harvest of blessings. Yet many who are claiming the promises of God for prosperity and "believing" God for money do not tithe and give offerings. But the Bible talks plainly about tithes and offerings.

Let's look at one passage along this line that's found in Proverbs chapter 3.

Honour the Lord with thy substance, and with the firstfruits of all thine increase:
So shall thy barns be filled with plenty, and thy presses shall burst out with new wine.

PROVERBS 3:9,10

These verses have to be applied and acted on along with the rest of the Word of God that we know concerning prosperity. Certainly, we need to conquer the giants that would try to keep us from entering our wealthy place. But with all of our claiming and confessing, we need to be honoring the Lord.

The word "honor" means *to respect* or *to pay tribute to.* When we act on verse 9, honoring the Lord with our giving, then we can confidently and expectantly claim the promise of verse 10: **"So shall thy BARNS be filled with PLENTY, and thy presses shall BURST OUT with new wine."**

Notice the word "barns" is plural. I like that, don't you? That's talking about more than one storehouse. I also like the words "plenty" and "burst out" because they remind me of an overflowing abundance.

They also remind me of Malachi 3:10, which says, **"Bring ye all the tithes into the storehouse, that there may be meat in mine house, and prove me now herewith, saith the Lord of hosts, if I will not open you the windows of heaven, and pour you out a blessing, THAT THERE SHALL NOT BE ROOM ENOUGH TO RECEIVE IT."**

That's talking about not having enough room to hold all the blessings. When you're walking in that mode, you just have to give somebody something — you've got so much! Your attitude is, *I'm loaded! I've got to give something away to lighten this load!*

Wouldn't you like to be able to say, "My wallet is getting too heavy. Lord, who do You want me to bless?"

As I said, claiming God's promises of prosperity is not enough to give you a financial breakthrough. You can speak the Word and just be parroting it. You could confess it until you turned blue and passed out! Just talking is not enough. Just talking will not sustain you in the hard times of tests and trials. You have to have some conviction behind your confession in order to make it!

Get Your Eyes Off Your Circumstances

For example, if you are experiencing poverty and lack, you need to get your eyes off your circumstances and begin focusing on the Word of God. You do that by meditating

on the Word (*see* Joshua 1:8 and Psalm 1:1 through 3).
Without meditating on the Word, your focus will be on
your bills, your debt, and your "broke" friends and
relatives!

But don't watch other people; watch Jesus. He is the
Author and Finisher of your faith (Heb. 12:2). If you
watch people, you may end up in the same mess some of
them are in. They don't know where they're going, and if
you follow them, you will become confused and
disheartened.

So faith in God's Word is involved in a financial
breakthrough, but so is obedience to the Word. I'm
talking about honoring God with your money in paying
tithes and giving offerings.

No money crosses the threshold of the doors in my
home without ten percent of it — the tithe — being
earmarked for God. That's part of what I mean about
honoring God.

Some people want to argue about the tithe. But, really,
they need to give God control over one hundred percent
of their money. If they did that, they wouldn't argue
about the tithe. They'd be paying the Lord His ten percent
because His Word says, **"Bring ye all the TITHES into
the storehouse..."** (Mal. 3:10).

Proverbs 3:9 says, **"Honour the Lord with thy
substance...."** That's talking about money. Honor the Lord

with your money. This verse also says, **"...and with the firstfruits of all thine increase."**

God wants the firstfruits, not the leftovers. Some people pay the department store and *tip* God.

Look at that verse again: **"...with the firstfruits of all thine INCREASE."** What is "increase"? Well, I'll tell you what it's *not*. Borrowed money, such as a debt-consolidation loan, is not increase. It's *de*crease. Those loan officers try to make you feel good because you've reduced your monthly payments. But they put the "big interest" on you till there's no telling how much you're paying back to that loan company over the next several years. Yet you're happy because you got out of the heat, so to speak. That's not increase.

Levels of Increase Will Come In 'Due Season'

There are levels of receiving according to your levels of giving — according to how you honor the Lord. Galatians 6:7 says, **"...whatsoever a man soweth, that shall he also reap."**

Verse 9 says, **"And let us not be weary in well doing: for in DUE SEASON we shall reap, if we faint not."** One thing you don't have to worry about is whether or not your due season is going to come. If you haven't been weary in sowing, your due season is always going to come through. That's why they call it due season. It is a spiritual law.

There are certain laws set up in the Bible that apply to financial prosperity, such as the law of sowing and reaping or giving and receiving. We also call it seedtime and harvest. The Bible says about this law: **"While the earth remaineth, seedtime and harvest, and cold and heat, and summer and winter, and day and night SHALL NOT CEASE"** (Gen. 8:2).

We know that laws such as this one exist, but we can't apply them and make them come to pass in our lives by simply making positive confessions. No, we have to apply these laws scripturally. In other words, if we want to reap — if we want harvest time — then we have to sow seed. We can't just "confess" to reap.

Many Christians, even preachers, try to sidestep some of these laws and try to receive prosperity some other way. For example, sometimes you'll hear a television preacher talk about the fact that if viewers don't send in an offering, the program is going to go off the air.

I would never give money to someone who said something like that. If someone tells you he's going off the air if you don't give, don't send him an offering. If you do, you're sowing into unstable soil, because he's just told you that he might fail any day now. He might go off the air, and you're going to "go off" with him. You'll turn the TV on one day, and another preacher will be standing there in front of the camera. Your money will be gone, and you will become disheartened.

I heard one minister say, "It's just as easy to live off the top of the barrel as it is from the bottom." I want to support men and women of God like that!

Some Christians are frustrated because they are not receiving their financial breakthroughs; they are not entering in to their wealthy place. Some of them know the principles of faith and of believing they receive first before having (*see* Mark 11:24). But they aren't properly applying spiritual laws. Those spiritual laws are working against them, because they are not giving properly.

Others are tithing, giving, and being obedient to the Lord in their finances, but they are not using their faith properly. Once they meet the conditions, they don't know how to reap in faith by holding on to their convictions — their firm persuasion — in the hard times.

Some people have tithed faithfully for years, have read books and listened to tapes about prosperity. But nothing is happening. They've even tried gimmicks, such as sending in offerings to preachers in exchange for "holy water" that's supposed to give them their breakthrough. The preacher's been telling them the windows of Heaven are open (Mal. 3:10), but nothing's coming out of those windows for them!

Something is wrong somewhere. God meant what He said in His Word, and if we are following it, something should be happening. The Word should be working in our lives.

The Promises Are Contingent Upon the Principles

One answer to the problem of lack is this: Stop claiming the *promises* while failing to apply the *principles*. In other words, if you are not tithing and giving offerings, stop trying to claim financial prosperity, because divine prosperity is not going to happen for you.

God established certain principles in His Word, and He did it for a reason. He talks about the tithe, and that's important, but there's more to it than that. Some people just write their tithe check without even thinking about it. They are in a satisfied position in which they just go through the motions; their heart is not in it.

As I said, the tithe is not the end; it's just the beginning. Beyond that door is the giving of offerings — honoring the Lord with your substance (Prov. 3:9). As I said, that word "substance" is talking about money because that verse goes on to talk about increase.

Actually, honoring the Lord with your money is more than just honoring Him with the tithe. It's giving Him complete control of your money and letting Him talk to you about what He wants you to do with it.

Some people are so uptight and concerned about money that they won't turn loose of any of it, even if the Lord tells them to give it. Some will say, "But I am saving that money for retirement."

Listen, God will help you retire "right" — don't worry about that. He'll have you taking real trips instead of just going up the street or around the corner!

I remember when my wife and I first began stepping out in honoring the Lord with our money. We often had to give up money we had saved, because God told us to give it up. Sometimes we gave it, trembling, but we obeyed God, and I'm so glad we did. We've never regretted it, not for one minute, because God always brought us something better than what we'd given up. He always blessed and increased us.

Some people think God is trying to rob them when He asks them to turn loose of some money. But He is not robbing them; He is positioning them. Positioning them for what? To receive more.

Some people won't allow God to position them for greater blessings and rewards because they are afraid. They don't trust Him to get that money back to them. They are holding on tight to forty dollars when they could be enjoying more. That forty dollars won't even come close to meeting their need, yet they refuse to give it. They won't sow it; therefore, they tie God's hands in the reaping aspect.

Regardless of your income or what you possess, whether it is a large or a small amount, God expects you to honor Him with it.

Now let's focus on the reward associated with
Proverbs 3:9.

**Honour the Lord with thy substance, and with the
firstfruits of all thine increase:
So shall thy barns be filled with plenty, and thy
presses shall burst out with new wine.**

PROVERBS 3:9,10

The word "plenty" in this verse means *fullness;
abundance*. The Hebrew root word for plenty means *to
become satisfied*. As I mentioned before, the expression, "So
shall thy barns be filled with plenty," depicts the greatest
possible abundance.

When we honor the Lord with our substance, God
promises not only to supply our needs, but to bless us
with plenty — the greatest possible abundance.

God wants you living in a large place — a wealthy
place. He wants you to live in such a way that your
neighbors don't understand you. You're so blessed that
they can't figure out where the money's coming from —
you've got so much!

So we've learned that we don't have a right to expect to
reap God's blessings if we have not sown — if we have not
honored Him with our substance or with the firstfruits of
our increase. God is faithful to do His part and increase us,
but we have to be faithful to do our part, and that is to
honor Him.

Faithful in Finances

We have to be good stewards of that which God has given us. This is easy to do when we realize that we are not owners, but managers. We are given substance in this life to manage, not to hoard up unto ourselves. As we manage according to God's will, He will find us faithful and give us more to manage.

Moreover it is required in stewards, that a man be found faithful.

1 CORINTHIANS 4:2

According to this verse, is faithfulness optional? No, it is *required* that we be found faithful.

When it comes to wealth, we have to be faithful stewards. Some people don't want to associate faithfulness with finances because they've been burned in the past by charlatans who just want money and will use every kind of gimmick you can imagine to get people's money. So when the truth comes along — because there is a fine line between the truth and deception — they are shell-shocked, so to speak.

Ministers who are just looking for an offering are prostituting the real prosperity message and the people who are giving offerings to these men and women. For example, a pastor once told me, "A certain company wants to come in and train my people how to give and then take up an offering for the church. But they want a certain percentage of what's received."

I said, "Don't let them do it. That's spiritual rape. If you do it, your people will never be intimate with you again." That just came out of my spirit.

We need balance in this prosperity teaching. We need the anointing, not a formula. For example, don't just run down to the altar and throw money when the Lord didn't tell you or inspire you to do it. Let the anointing guide you, or you will get hurt.

Some Christians are getting unbalanced in the prosperity message, and they're doing all sorts of crazy things, such as quitting their jobs when the Lord didn't tell them to quit. They heard of somebody else quitting his job, so they quit theirs.

I worked a secular job sixteen years, and ten of those years, I was in the ministry. One day I was working on the job, and God told me, "Today is your day. I want you to quit."

My finances were in no different condition than they were the day before. I still had a lot of bills. But I'd heard from Heaven, so I was able to act in faith, not presumption and craziness.

So I quit just like the Lord told me. I put on my suit and went in to work and quit. I was too young for retirement benefits. I just left it all behind.

My boss said to me, "What are you going to do now?" I said, "The Lord is going to take care of me." My boss ended up moving into the same neighborhood I live in now. He often passes my house as he's riding his bicycle. As my boss, he used to make more money than me. But I got hold of the Word and got on God's system. I tell you, no job can pay you enough compared to God's system. There is just something about honoring God with your finances that will put you over far more than any job could.

When my wife and I wanted to build the house we're in, we went in to see the banker at a certain mortgage company. He had a plush office and lived in a plush home. He didn't want to lend us the money, because he said the house we wanted to build was too big for the area where we wanted to live.

The president of that company asked me, "Why do you want to build a house like that?"

I answered, "Because I'm the president of a company too. You're a company president, and *you* live in a nice house in that area. Why do you have the kind of house *you* have?"

We eventually got our loan somewhere else, and that first mortgage company we went to went out of business. Afterward, I saw that man in the neighborhood one day, and he looked bad. He'd lost his health, his business, and he was losing his house and his cars.

Now I was by no means rejoicing over this man's misfortune, but I knew what had happened. He came against me when I was getting ready to build my house — a house the Lord actually told me to build. He "touched" God's anointed (1 Chron. 16:22; Ps. 105:15), and it cost him.

You know, that promise God made to Abraham is valid today with God's people. God is a covenant-keeper. He told Abraham, "... I will bless them that bless thee, and curse him that curseth thee. . . " (Gen. 12:3).

Every person who put his hand on me to come against me failed to prosper. He or she "went down" financially.

Now that didn't happen because I'm anybody special. The same is true for you. Whoever blesses you, God will bless. Whoever attacks you will not prosper. When the Bible talks about not touching God's anointed, that's talking about you and me — about all God's covenant people. If you are carrying yourself right — if you are living right according to His Word — then you are honoring the Lord. (Honoring the Lord doesn't just mean honoring Him with your money, although honoring God with your money is part of it, and it's good and right.)

Honoring the Lord is very important; it puts you in another category — a category of blessings. Honoring the Lord with your money puts you in a category of financial blessing.

On the other hand, we cannot expect God to deliver us out of financial bondage and prosper and bless us when we fail to be good stewards of what He has given us.

Some people think that good stewardship is giving money to someone with a frayed, tight suit on that's out of style and shiny because it's been ironed so much. Certainly, we are to take care of the poor, and there is a blessing in obeying God in that area and caring for the needs of the poor. But the Bible also talks about sowing into good ground. You reap a good harvest when you sow into good ground. The people and ministries you sow into don't have to be broke. In fact, they *shouldn't* be broke! The Bible also talks about the fact that more shall be given to the one who has something (*see* Matthew 25:29). One minister calls it giving "upward." I believe that when you *give* "up," you *go* "up."

There is financial blessing in honoring the Lord with your money and doing with your substance what He tells you to do. Obedience, faith, and honor are the keys. If you will stick with the Lord and His Word and persevere in these three areas of obedience, faith, and honor, a financial breakthrough awaits you, and you find your wealthy place!

About the Author

Dr. Leroy Thompson Sr. is the pastor and founder of Word of Life Christian Center in Darrow, Louisiana, a growing and thriving body of believers from various walks of life. He has been in the ministry for twenty-two years, serving for twenty years as a pastor. Even though he completed his undergraduate degree and theology doctorate and was an instructor for several years at a Christian Bible college in Louisiana, it wasn't until 1983, when he received the baptism in the Holy Spirit, that the revelation knowledge of God's Word changed his life, and and it continues to increase his ministry. Dr. Thompson attributes the success of his life and ministry to his reliance on the Word of God and to being filled with the Holy Spirit and led by the Spirit of God. Today Dr. Thompson travels across the United States taking the message of ministerial excellence, dedication, and discipline to the Body of Christ.

Other Books by Dr. Leroy Thompson Sr.

Money Cometh to the Body of Christ!

The Voice of Jesus:
Speaking God's Word With Authority

What To Do When Your Faith Is Challenged

Money, Thou Art Loosed!

To order,
write or call:

Ever Increasing Word Ministries
P. O. Box 7
Darrow, LA 70725

1 (888) 238-WORD
(9673)

To contact Dr. Leroy Thompson Sr.,
write:

Dr. Leroy Thompson Sr.
Ever Increasing Word Ministries
P. O. Box 7
Darrow, Louisiana 70725

Please include your prayer requests
and comments when you write.

To obtain a free catalog of Dr. Thompson's teaching materials
or to receive a free quarterly newsletter, write to the address above.